COMPETITIVE OPPORTUNITY

COMPETITIVE OPPORTUNITY

How to Achieve Superior Performance in Difficult Times

RUPERT HART

KOGAN PAGE

With grateful thanks to

Sue Black
Kate Stedman
Mark Melling
Mike Woodhouse
Neil Hart

First published in 1992

Kogan Page Limited
120 Pentonville Road
London N1 9JN

British Library Cataloguing in Publication Data

A CIP record for this book is available from the British Library.

ISBN 0-7494-0612-7

Printed and bound in Great Britain by Clays Ltd, St Ives plc

CONTENTS

Preface

Where there's chaos there's opportunity.

Competitive Opportunity will inspire you to see and exploit the very real opportunities in difficult economic conditions. It contains a comprehensive review of creative techniques presented in a readable way. The proven concepts which have been distilled from the many examples of companies that have been successful should be useful in augmenting your own experience.

Aimed at general managers and those wanting a business-wide view of strategy in a downturn, the book will prove especially useful to managers who have perhaps not been exposed to such challenges before.

The many ideas presented here are applicable not only to difficult economic conditions, such as a recession and the lingering recovery afterwards, but also to industry-specific downturns. (I have used the generic term 'downturn' to denote a period of stagnant demand where the exact nature of its cause is not important.) They should therefore be helpful in deciding what to do to handle maturing markets, overcapacity and price wars.

Companies who have suffered in the past will want to make sure that they take advantage of the opportunities in the next difficult period. This book will help them to prepare.

While some are wringing their hands, others with a different attitude are taking advantage of the challenge. This book is for those people.

Rupert Hart

Note

Masculine pronouns have been used throughout this book. This stems from a desire to avoid ugly and cumbersome language, and no discrimination, prejudice or bias is intended.

Part I
Adversity Stimulates Improvement

Chapter 1

An Ocean of Opportunity

Downturns are tough times. Competitive pressures are greater. Yet few are aware of the many opportunities available in these difficult periods. One of the key messages of this book is that 'the cleverly expressed opposite of any generally accepted idea is worth a fortune'.

The past is another country

The nature of modern Western business is such that as winter follows summer, and as night follows day, so recessions and downturns follow booms. Customers' preferences and priorities change, competitive pressures increase enormously, and profits fall into a vice. Eventually, boom times will reappear. Such cycles are an inevitable part of business life.

Companies which fail to plan for the end of a boom or the end of a downturn should expect to be usurped by those which do. Time and tide wait for no man. The winners in such times of competitive opportunity are those which can adapt to the realities of the marketplace and accept that, like tides and time itself, some elements of cycles are too big for them to control.

Recessions set the stage for the boom periods which follow. Those who win through will be better placed to take advantage of the upturn when it comes.

However, as the previous recession and recovery occurred over a decade ago, many people have not been exposed to the level of decision-making required in such demanding times, while few people learned and successfully applied the lessons. John Kenneth Galbraith, the well-known economic historian and authority on stock market crashes, believes that 'financial memory is about ten years. This is about the time between one episode of sophisticated stupidity and the next.'

When managing in a downturn this lack of experience in such changed conditions can often lead to missed opportunities. As an analogy, consider the tale of an experiment on the effect of hiring inexperienced personnel for trading on the stock market. In a simulated marketplace the newcomers would bid up the prices into a boom which would quickly develop into a bust. A second time it would happen again. But by the third time the patterns of trading would calm down to a gentle see-saw, and the excesses of inexperience would have been blown away.

Such times show up bad management. Competitors, technology and distribution channels have moved on. Yet there is no greater constriction on creative thought than the history of past successes. The opportunity lies in using the situation to put the house in order and gain competitive advantage over those competitors who have not.

A time of competitive opportunity

Competitive pressures can increase substantially in a downturn. Revenues plummet and everybody is fighting to maintain or increase their slice of the cake. Successful companies are not crushed by the prospect but look for the opportunities. Companies who are alert and ready to make the appropriate moves can dramatically improve their relative competitive position. Many great competitive positions have been established in a downturn. Indeed, industry slumps are about the only time competitors can be completely eliminated.

Companies should never lose sight of the competitive realities of the marketplace. It was Israel's Golda Meir who declared of her embattled nation that 'we intend to remain alive. Our neighbours want to see us dead. This is not a question that leaves much room for compromise.'

This book espouses the surprisingly rarely used combination of rational cost-cutting and real strengthening of marketing. By marrying a continuing drive for productive efficiency with carefully chosen market strategies a company becomes even more formidable in bad times than in the fat years.

Many of these actions are of course applicable to times other than a downturn. Yet it is an inescapable fact of both human and corporate life that adversity often provides the essential stimulus to action. These actions can be grouped into three categories, around which the structure of this book is based.

1. Only in a downturn does a manager have the greatest possible mandate to put his house in order, to cut costs, and to increase flexibility. With lower costs and greater flexibility, he can make more profit, or he can use this enormous competitive advantage to wage a powerful war against his competitors.
2. Recessions also allow companies to change the rules. People both inside and outside the company are more receptive to change at such

times so that previous ways of doing business can be changed with less aggravation to trading partners or competitors. Enormous advantages lie in wait for the person able to understand customers' new needs, and to supply solutions to those needs better than the competition.

3. Towards the end of a downturn and its recovery period the combination of competitors' mistakes and inaction, the gathering of your company's resources, and the weakening of competitors by your company's marketing, can lead to your company being able to acquire or eliminate a former competitor, to buy assets cheaply, or to merge with a firm providing complementary products.

It is because business life is so complex that in order to systematize the concepts I have had to simplify and subdivide them. In reality, you will have to combine them in a unique way to suit your company and its situation.

Be pro-active

Most people hibernate in a recession. They talk of 'battening down the hatches', 'getting back to basics', 'retrenchment'. They become introverted, 'keep their heads down', and don't look around. We'll 'stick to our knitting', they say, in order to 'ride out the recession'. This is not pro-active leadership!

Downturns provide much opportunity: opportunity not available to any such extent in boom times. Then is the time for action to exploit the competitive opportunity.

Chapter 2

Leadership Is the Key

In a crisis, there is much confusion, uncertainty and fear. It is the function of the leader to provide direction, certainty and reassurance. The success or fate of a company often rests in the hands of the leadership.

Now that many companies have moved towards decentralizing decision-making to the lowest position at which a competent decision can be made, we all become keystones in the construction of an enduring organizational structure. The lessons here therefore apply to all of us.

Leaders are made in a crisis. Helping to guide a company through a downturn should be seen as a real challenge, not a crisis to be fled from but a quality to be actively sought out as an important constituent in a manager's personal and professional development.

A highly motivated person, as we all know, works three times harder than a clock-watcher. A leader must therefore show how people's personal goals can be allied to that of the company to bring out the very best in them. In the words of Sir John Harvey-Jones, former chairman of ICI, one of the world's largest chemical manufacturers, 'leadership is enabling ordinary people to achieve extraordinary things. Almost anyone can do anything they believe they can do. The trouble is most of us believe we can't do things.' Building hope and inspiring the team is perhaps the most important role of the leader.

Now it should come as no surprise that war veterans talk of their war years throughout their lives: they were inspired to be all they could be. Similarly, a crisis may provide present employees with their finest hour.

Leading people in a business crisis is in some ways harder than in war. For, in business, unlike war, people are apt to scramble off the sinking ship and managers, unlike admirals, cannot use the threat of shooting to prevent desertion. Holding on to valued employees therefore requires a good understanding of their viewpoint. Only then is it possible to produce reasons which can persuade them to stay.

Everybody wants security of some sort, and nobody wants to be tainted with the stigma of a lost cause. So for people to remain with a company in crisis, they have to believe the cause to be worthwhile. For instance, employees can be persuaded that the experience will be useful in their personal development. They fight on if they feel they would let their friends down by leaving, and especially if they have nowhere else to go. Selling such a vision to employees is the very essence of the leader. The success of the Body Shop, the UK cosmetics retailing chain, for instance, has often been attributed to the approach to business of the chief executive Anita Roddick. The human potential of the individuals working in the organization is released because they all have the same vision.

Without a vision, the people perish

A good wartime officer will always make sure that all of his men understand the goal and the strategy to reach it. They must be motivated to play their part in the worthwhile cause, and to understand their role in achieving it. In this way, if a crisis decision has to be made by the leader, the men will understand the context in which it has to be made, and will be calmed by the logic. They will follow the leader if they trust him and his motives. For them to do this, they need to believe that the leader has their best interests at heart and is competent to lead them. Sir John Harvey-Jones believes that 'management is about knowing where you want to get to, driving like hell to get there and forcing people to go with you by making the objective totally clear'.

Our perceptions are often coloured by the situation we find ourselves in. If things are bad, for instance, we think they're going to get worse. Leaders must reverse this, and build hope. It would be hard to find a better example of this leadership than Field Marshal Montgomery who, with Patton and Bradley, led the assaults into Europe after D-Day. As victor of the battle of El Alamein in 1942, he was the author of the first real reversal of the allies' fortunes. Montgomery was sent over to North Africa to take over a dispirited British Eighth Army which had suffered defeat after defeat at the hands of Rommel. Montgomery built enormous hope in the troops by declaring that there would be no more retreat, and by persuading them to believe that they could defeat the Germans. He reconstructed morale by making them take pride in themselves – by intense physical training and countless exercises. He led them to trust him by devising a workable strategy. A decisive victory was won at El Alamein which laid the foundations for a resurgence of effort and ultimate triumph a few years later.

The leader must communicate his strategy and objectives clearly and openly in order to avoid the team pulling in different directions and wastefully dissipating energy. He must paint a vista of what will be, and then plot the road map for getting there. Communication of the objectives is a critical element in leadership.

Communicate! Communicate! Communicate!

It is the opinion of the great turnaround artist of the US, Marvin Davis, that communication is *the* key priority of any leader in a crisis. Proper awareness of a credible recovery plan can play a key part in persuading good quality waverers who are about to leave the sinking ship to stay. However, communication should be a two-way process: it is well known that people support what they help to achieve. Discussions and input from employees help them to identify personally with the plan.

The success of the open communication approach is exemplified by the turnarounds at Burger King and Detroit Trim. Barry Gibbons, widely credited with the dramatic turnaround of Burger King for Grand Metropolitan, feels that 'underneath people want to believe. You can succeed with the people on hand if you make it clear what you need from them.'

When Detroit Trim, a small company making car upholstery for Chrysler, was threatened with shutdown because its products could be bought cheaper elsewhere, it took on Charles Howell, an Arthur D Little consultant. He was able to save the company, turn it around and improve productivity by 25 per cent. He attributed this to his willingness to share information, to answer any questions and to build trust. In contrast, 'ultimatums and hardball tactics', he insisted, 'get plants shut down'.

You have to communicate goals in a way that the employees understand the relevance to them. So many companies embark on an expensive and often ultimately fruitless task of writing a mission statement, realigning their focus and changing their corporate logo. Yet their mission statement, a public declaration of the vision and the goals of the company, too often emerges as just another 'bit of puffery'. A 'Big Four' bank in the UK, for example, declared in its mission statement the goal of 'maximizing return on equity'. How, asked an industry observer, could the person on the cash till relate to that?

Goals are therefore entirely useless unless you can make them so clear that everyone understands them and can do something about them every day. They are essential in setting quantifiable targets. Goals must be accepted whole-heartedly throughout the organization so that employees can count on management support for their decisions based on their interpretation of the organization's goals.

It is a common fallacy that crises leave no time for communication and consensus-building. People think of officers in wartime giving orders without discussion and expecting unquestioning obedience. That is not so. People abhor uncertainty more than anything else. That is why communication is so critical.

All for one, and one for all

The leader must be in touch with the feelings of his troops in order to answer their concerns and to influence them towards the desired goal. There is no substitute to 'management by walking around', as opposed to 'strut and tut'.

The so damaging confrontational 'us' and 'them' attitude must not be allowed to survive and to get in the way of mutual progress. This was recognized at Detroit Trim by Charles Howell. He managed to persuade the union that only fully coordinated action between them would save the company. A year later the slimmed-down company was taking on more and more work from Chrysler, at much reduced cost. Working together had succeeded. As the chairman of the United Auto Workers shop committee at the plant said: 'What used to be their business is now our business too.'

Of all the demands placed on a leader of an organization in a downturn, that of building hope is surely the most critical. Such a quality will never be so important as in straitened times. Personal example and demonstrating an all-in-it-together attitude are important pointers the leader can provide for his co-workers. It would be hard to find a better example of this attitude than Lee Iacocca at Chrysler. In the early 1980s, Chrysler was in crisis. Number three player in the US, its cars weren't selling while the Japanese sold the products that customers really wanted to buy. Losses were mounting alarmingly. Plants were shut down, workforces axed and pay cut. Lee Iacocca, the chief executive officer, recognized that equality of sacrifice sends a powerful message. He requested that his salary be dropped from $360,000 to just $1. Only then did he feel able to look union negotiators in the eye. Who would not follow such a man who, by his example, showed that everybody was in it together?

One of the important demands on leadership is judgement based on knowledge of market conditions. The background is now set in Chapter 3.

Chapter 3

Learning From the Past

'People always think it will be different this time around', declared investment fund manager Bob Beckman. Yet, by looking at previous recessions, several common threads and techniques can be found which can be managed opportunistically to good effect. Although we do not know how to predict accurately the onset of a downturn or the depth of economic hardship, or even the detailed effects on markets and individual companies, the little knowledge available can provide dividends: 'In the country of the blind, the one-eyed man is king'. This chapter therefore attempts to provide some background to market conditions.

The effects of recession

The first characteristic of a recession is a severe downturn in market demand. Some markets suffer almost cardiac arrest. For firms which have experienced a decade of only increasing incomes, such new conditions prove to be a great shock and can have devastating effects. For instance, individual companies around the world suffered badly in the recession of the early 1990s, as the following declines in profits reported in 1990 and 1991 show: Whirlpool profits were down 65 per cent; Renault suffered a 65 per cent fall; Mead Paper profits dropped 34 per cent; Sears Merchandise Group reported a 63 per cent decline in income; Olivetti was down 41 per cent; Wimpey Construction dropped 72 per cent; and the profits of one of the UK's largest banks, National Westminster, fell from £1.4 billion to £0.4 billion. Smaller companies also suffered, with last-ditch county court judgements on winding-up orders up 64 per cent in the UK.

High street retailers, riding a wave of consumer demand, never foresaw the end to the boom. Stores which had got used to a growth rate of 7 to 8 per cent in the consumer spending spree of the mid to late 1980s found the stagnant conditions of the following recession trying. Having budgeted for that sort of rate of increase to continue, they allowed their cost bases to rise. Some thought that the flourishing consumer spending would never collapse, and that opening more and more shops was the way to ever-greater profits. With hindsight, it is easy to see that this was a 'very silly period', as one stock analyst described it. A combination of stagnant volumes and flaccid pricing meant that retailers' revenues rose at a much slower rate than their costs, therefore squeezing their margins.

An even more disastrous case was that of mechanical engineering, which is very sensitive to the cycles of companies' investment plans. In the UK, during the recession in the early 1990s, manufacturing investment fell 24 per cent.

We can see therefore that recessions and downturns can have a severe effect on industries and individual companies. Understanding the reasons for these effects requires further understanding of the nature of such economic shocks.

What exactly is a recession?

Economic recessions are formally defined as a decline in gross national product (GNP) for two consecutive quarters.

It can be shown from past data that economic recessions tend to happen every six years or so. This is not a regular cycle, however, and its variability has been high in the past. In the UK, for example, since the end of the Second World War until the recession of the early 1980s, the period between booms was 4½ years on average, with typically 33 months downturn and 22 months upswing. Yet the 1980s were the time of almost decade-long growth, a period which has given the lie to such 'precise' figures.

If the length of a recession is hard to predict, then its depth is even more so. The average decline from the peak of a boom to the trough of a recession for the previous eight recessions since the Second World War has been shown to be 2.6 per cent of GNP, but again this is highly variable.

A recession's effect on individual companies, as we have seen, tends to be much more accentuated than that of a boom.

Recessions are usually started by shocks which suddenly reduce the purchasing power of some sector of the economy. Energy prices provided the shock for the 1974 UK and US recessions by severely cutting purchasing power. Monetary contraction cut demand to initiate the recessions of the early 1980s.

The depth of a recession is also affected dramatically by business and consumer confidence. The UK stock market crash in October 1987 and again two years later badly hit the essential confidence required to make spending continue.

Recessions are hard to predict. They can occur even when the long-term trend is upwards, and when the economic growth rate is high. Recessions have also become much more global in nature, affecting not just one country but many.

Most people think only of economic recessions which affect the whole economy. But there are also industry downturns which may occur independently of economic recessions – they have much in common and many useful responses are provided throughout the book as examples.

Hard-to-spot turning points

The points at which the economy slides into a recession, or out of it, are notoriously difficult to pinpoint. De-stocking is usually seen as the harbinger of a recession as manufacturers run down their stocks to supply demand rather than increasing production.

Recognizing that the onset of a recession is critically dependent on business and consumer spending, the press and the government watch key indicators of confidence carefully. In the US, one of the most commonly quoted is the National Association of Purchasing Managers' confidence index, where purchasing managers are asked whether they expect to buy more or less in the next period. The balance of the responses produces a percentage rating: above 50 per cent indicates confidence of greater spending; below 50 per cent, pessimism. In the UK, this function is taken up by the Confederation of British Industry's employers' confidence index.

The end of a recession is usually considered to occur when consumers lead the economy by increasing their spending levels. Their confidence is thought to depend on their opinions of their future prospects and their chances of avoiding the still-lengthening unemployment queues. Households often fuel a spending spree by running down their savings or increasing their credit borrowing. Hence recovery tends to depend on the level of their savings and of their debt.

Poor statistics

One of the reasons for the limited understanding of, and belated response to, the phases of a recession is the nature of the statistics available.

Governments, for instance, have no other way of guiding the ship of state but by looking at the wake. The delay in producing statistics, and their poor ability to reflect underlying conditions, is such that by the time the official observers point out that the economy is in recession, the country, and your company, is already suffering it. Indeed, it was found in 1991 that statistics on the growth of the US economy, which had been produced six months previously, had been overstated by almost a fifth. Clearly, the economy had been significantly more sluggish than previously thought.

Yet this is the information that governments have to use in their management of the economy. Despite our belief in free markets, governments do play a key part. Unfortunately, even with such imperfect information, and despite the reams of data run through elaborate models, many observers admit that economists just don't know very much about what makes the economy tick.

Politics affects economics

Many forecasters have a vested interest in influencing policy, and hence their projections have to be taken with a pinch of salt. If a government can find even the tiniest scrap of evidence that the economy is sliding into a shallow downturn, rather than a recession, it will protest its case vigorously. Similarly with any signs of recovery. It will always be determinedly optimistic because it wants to encourage businesses to invest, consumers to spend and voters to ignore allegations that it has mismanaged the economy. Employers' organizations and opposition parties will of course tend to lean the other way.

The 'R'-word is so emotionally charged that governments the world over are loath to even breathe it. In France the administration responded to such taunts by declaring a 'ralentissement' (a slowing-down) rather than a full-blown 'recession'.

Since it is no secret that voters are influenced more by the state of the economy than by anything else, it should come as no surprise that governments frequently concentrate on short-term improvements in the economy just before an election. The price for these benefits has to be paid afterwards; history shows that recovery after a recession tends to be slowed by post-election setbacks, such as increased unemployment.

The experts are often mistaken

As proof that even the best-informed authorities can often be in considerable error, I present two illustrations.

Professor Garel Rhys is an expert on motor industry economics for the UK's Society of Motor Manufacturers and Traders. He was quoted as saying in August 1990 that the economy as a whole 'could slip into a recession early next year. But I don't think it will affect the motor industry much . . . I don't think it will get worse next year.' Yet less than a year later, with some observers claiming that the recession was the worst since the 1930s, vehicle manufacturers were openly announcing 10 per cent drops in list prices, with many customers reporting that they were able to achieve a 25 per cent discount.

A survey in the *Wall Street Journal* by the National Association of Business Economists in February 1990 said 60.6 per cent of the 65 members polled did not expect a recession before 1993. Yet the US was later acknowledged in official US government statistics to have entered recession in July 1990. That's not three years but just five months later.

It is likely that forecasters feel they have an obligation to demonstrate a very positive viewpoint because confidence has an important effect on business. When people believe that the economy is going to deteriorate or stay in the doldrums, they have a fair chance of being right since it is their investment decisions which cause it to be so.

Interest rates rise

Throughout the world, history shows that interest rates tend to rise in a recession, often doubling and staying high for some time afterwards. For companies, this tends to have two direct effects. The first is that demand for 'big ticket' items will be severely curtailed. Second, debt repayments will become a much more significant proportion of cash flow than in the past.

Control over interest rates, either by an independent central bank or by an overtly politically controlled bank, has for some time been seen as the primary tool in combatting inflation and 'overheating' of the economy. Inflation will only be checked when employers and workers are afraid to pursue the restoration of their real incomes because of growing unemployment, bankruptcies and depression of trade. A government committed to fighting inflation is therefore likely to keep interest rates high in order to curtail rising prices, even if the economy requires stimulation.

Today, when currency exchange rates are more dependent on flows of capital than trade flows, interest rates are also used as a means to bolster a nation's exchange rate. Interest rates are increased to encourage investors to invest in the country. Here, it is the differential of the interest rate relative to competing nations which matters. If one country were to keep its interest rate high to stifle its domestic inflation, another might find it difficult to reduce its rate to ease the burden on domestic debtors. Hence, interest rates and the cash flow of highly leveraged companies have become increasingly vulnerable to extra-national factors.

Interest rates have an important effect on the demand for 'big ticket' goods and services. Companies making industrial capital equipment purchases are forced to think rather harder about how the increased cost of money changes their payback periods, and increases their risk. In the consumer arena, expensive goods purchased with high levels of debt –

houses for example – may require so large an outlay on regular interest payments as to curtail demand severely.

A typical example of a supplier suffering from these knock-on effects is Coloroll, the UK manufacturer of household products, such as carpets, glassware and furniture, which entered into receivership in 1990. Once the darling of the UK stock market, it was the victim of the so-called 'double whammy' of lower demand for its 'big ticket' products and increased interest payments on its acquisition debt caused by elevated interest rates.

In a downturn the margin of error between profit and loss is much reduced as sales fall to find costs rising to meet them. For a highly leveraged firm, interest repayments may well become a significant charge on the bottom line. Hence, coordination of incoming and outgoing money becomes a priority – few banks will support even a short cash-flow deficit. Most companies ultimately fail because of lack of cash flow.

Eventually, interest rates fall, but they can often stay high for extended periods. Furthermore, interest rates may not always be immediately reduced for all customers: where companies are unable to have their loans financed elsewhere, or where the risk profile of a firm is considered to warrant it, rates have sometimes even been increased. Therefore, the pressure on companies from debt repayment can remain for some time after the statistics state otherwise.

The spectre of 'stagflation', of poor demand overshadowed by high inflation, has receded since its common appearance in the late 1970s as governments have come to understand the corrosive effect of inflation and have raised the priority for keeping it under control. Inflation particularly affects valuation of inventory, cash flow, business risk and planning horizons, and squeezes margins.

Why so great an effect on your company?

We have seen that the nation's output only falls a few per cent yet individual company performance indicates much greater sensitivity to a downturn. It is important to understand the basis for this.

First, in most countries, government spending, which is relatively insensitive to recessions, tends to represent about a half of the economy. Hence, the private sector will experience at least twice the decline seen by the economy as a whole.

Second, a crucial influence on a company's profits is its level of fixed costs. If these are a high proportion of total costs, then the company's profits are highly sensitive to a downturn in demand. For this reason, it has been quite common to see companies announcing falls in profits which are much sharper than that of their sales. Renault, the French state-owned automotive group, for example, suffered a 65.4 per cent drop in pre-tax profits in the first half of 1991 while its turnover fell only 6 per cent.

The multiplier and accelerator

There are two other important influences on the business cycle: the multiplier and the accelerator. These help to explain the extent and timing of an industry sector's downturn compared to the position of the economy as a whole.

The multiplier effect shows that every pound spent tends to multiply through the economy as the pound passes through people's hands. This means that your business is sensitive to the original source of money. So, even if the economy turns down only a few per cent, your company's revenues may well decrease further.

The knock-on effect cascades throughout the economy. Part of this multiplier effect is due to the fact that the failure of a large company may well knock out many smaller companies. John Kenneth Galbraith describes it in a more earthy manner by relating an old Canadian saying that when the horse dies on the street the oats no longer pass through for the sparrows.

As an economy slows down, its rate of growth in productivity tails off. The accelerator effect is the name given to the process by which this leads to a decline in all sectors of the economy. Since an ever-growing rate of productivity is impossible, the consensus is that the accelerator effect tends to ensure that a boom cannot continue for ever and that a downturn will ensue.

For companies the significance of the multiplier and accelerator effects is that market demand in a given sector is quite sensitive to external pressures, that it could lag the economy by a significant period, and that cyclical downturns are ultimately inevitable.

After-effects linger

The violent aftershocks of a downturn continue to shake up business for some time after the bottom is reached. Upswings, when they come, are seldom sharp and of sustained growth.

Like a car reaching the end of a curve with too much speed and having to brake and skid violently to avoid falling off a precipice, the worst effects of a downturn are often reserved for the later stages. Companies which have soldiered along, trying to make it through, finally give up exhausted, having expended all their resources. Four years after the official end of a previous US recession, for instance, American factories ranging from textile plants in North Carolina to machine-tool plants in Ohio were still closing their doors.

'Those who forget the past are condemned to repeat it.' George Santayana was a philosopher who is perhaps best remembered for this famous saying. There will always be companies which fail to heed this advice and this provides opportunities for companies which have some understanding of the business environment in which they work.

Part II
Costs, Flexibility and Cash

The following chapters explain what is required to exploit to the full the competitive opportunities available from a thorough reappraisal of the internal workings of a company.

Chapter 4 covers the importance of being objective and provides techniques for bringing down the organization's costs. Chapter 5 is concerned with the flexibility of a company. It includes methods for improving the company's break-even position, and concentrates on employee productivity, the prime source of flexibility in any company. Chapter 6 outlines some unusual aspects of cash control and the opportunities available there.

Opportunities

After ten years, organizations build up an accretion of barnacles on their hull and need a jolly good scrape.

Robert Horton, Chairman, BP

Recession and recovery provide great opportunities

John Sculley, chairman of Apple Computers, commenting on the revival of Apple's fortunes after the 1985 computer industry downturn, described the advantages of a crisis in his autobiography: 'It creates an environment in which executives have the greatest chance to make significant changes in a company . . . And how much support can one expect from the company's shareholders, suppliers, and customers if an executive radically alters the company when it's not in a state of crisis?'

Much can be achieved in difficult conditions which cannot otherwise normally be attempted. Toyota is a prime example of this. If its severe cash-flow problems hadn't necessitated a rapid reduction in working capital, it would probably not have instituted its famous just-in-time method, and would perhaps not have become the worldbeater it is today.

This example shows that an important opportunity presented by a difficult trading period is to overcome the 'if it ain't broke, don't fix it' syndrome which is prevalent in boom times. All companies need to undergo a process of steady incremental improvements in order to keep ahead of the competition.

A mandate to cut costs

At no other time in the business cycle will a manager have such a mandate to cut costs. As Lee Iacocca, chairman of Chrysler and architect of its dramatic turnaround, was to say: 'There is nothing better than a life and death struggle to help get your priorities straight.'

Like presidents of Brazil, the manager of a company in crisis is seen as having the right to impose an austerity programme. If people have to be let go, then that is perceived as a legitimate way of improving the survival chances of the company and its remaining employees.

The continual hunt for sales growth throughout a long boom period will tend to mask the enormous waste and excess inside any company. In straitened times, however, a controlled diet is called for.

In the eyes of T Boone Pickens, the oil baron of Mesa Petroleum, 'organizations get fat and lazy. Particularly when they have been feeding off of a fat cash cow for years.'

The deficiencies of badly managed business units and products can be glossed over during a period of growth when even abysmally controlled activities can earn profits. But such deficiencies become plainly apparent in a downturn. Even efficient, well-managed retailing businesses, such as Sainsbury's, have shut down several stores whose performance fell short of what was required.

If it's broke, fix it quick

'In the long run we are all dead', wrote John Kenneth Galbraith, the eminent economic historian. In the same way, we need to keep an eye on the urgent and short term, and not just those factors which will prove important in the long term. If you're painting a house to protect it from the seasons, for example, you would still put down your paintbrush and pick up a fire bucket if the house caught fire. Hence, you need to respond quickly to areas which need urgent attention.

Downturns tend to expose poor performance and are excellent opportunities to make those painful decisions which have been put off for so long. If an activity is bleeding red ink, management has to consider carefully whether it will ever generate worthwhile profit, and whether the management time and cash can be spared right now to fix it. If not, the haemorrhage has to be stopped right away and the business unit shut down. The axe has to fall on products, services, regions, salespeople, customers, distribution channels, suppliers, and all activities which will never pay their way or which cannot be turned around quickly. It is a preoccupation with efficiency, stretching across company departmental boundaries, during the recovery period which characterizes superlative companies.

There will be no better opportunity to realign the focus of the company, cut costs and improve the flexibility than during a downturn and its recovery period. At the end of the difficult times the company will emerge lean, mean and hungry – a formidable competitive machine.

Chapter 4

Cut Costs Strategically

Cutting costs is one of the most important opportunities of a downturn, and is often one of the first activities. However, the need to avoid damage to the healthy muscle of the company requires an understanding of the key principles of cost reduction. Managers must first get the facts on which to set realistic targets. Then, when they make the cuts required, they should look to the future in order to avoid reducing strategically important expenditure. That is the essence of this chapter.

Key principles

Focusing on the essentials

'If you try to catch two rabbits at the same time you'll not catch either', relates a Japanese proverb. With that in mind the military historian Liddell Hart expounded on the parallels between warfare and business. 'Every military operation must be directed towards a clearly defined, decisive, and attainable objective.' In other words, the leader needs to define simply and singly where the company is going. 'One rule of thumb that I've learned', said a pharmaceutical executive, 'is to know to the bottom of my soul what it is I am trying to accomplish.'

The scalpel not the bacon-slicer

If a patient requires surgery, the surgeon does not take off little pieces from each part of the entire body but applies the scalpel only to the diseased organ. In the same way, asking every cost centre for across-the-board cuts of 10 per cent may demonstrate equality of sacrifice throughout the company but does not solve the problem. Worse, such 'equality of misery' misses the opportunity of removing fat from overweight departments and instead cuts into healthy muscle. Take the opportunity to remodel the organization in a healthier, trimmer image.

Linkages are important

Not only do some departments contribute more to a company's profits than others, but cutting costs in one area can actually increase the total costs because of interrelated costs. The 10 per cent approach mentioned above represents a short-sighted failure to recognize such linkages. Michael Porter, Professor at Harvard Business School, illustrates this point with reference to Canon photocopiers, which found that it could substantially reduce the manufactured cost of its copiers by, perhaps surprisingly, purchasing higher priced parts. Since these were of much more consistent size and of a simpler design, the new parts were able virtually to eliminate the need for the labour-intensive adjustment previously required. Cutting individual component costs in this case would in fact have been detrimental to the overall product cost because of a neglect of the linkages throughout the production process.

Purchasing departments' activities are often restricted to processing orders and obtaining goods at the lowest possible price. Yet purchasing departments would be better used if they had a hand in developing suppliers, in product design and in all aspects of material management. In this way, they would exploit the creative benefits of linkages to cut costs.

Information is the key

You can't fix what you can't measure

'A journey of a thousand leagues begins with a single step', wrote the sage Lao-Tzu. The first step in making use of a downturn as an opportunity to slim down is to diagnose the basis of the problem. Analyze the position, compare it with where the company wants to be, and then take action to join the two.

The collection of quantitative information – for marketing, motivation and costing – should be a normal part of business operations, even if it is difficult to place a financial value on it. Using quantifiable information avoids woolly statements and provides an objective basis for comparison.

Get the facts

It is truly amazing how many executives actually do not know key statistics about their responsibilities. They work on intuition and what has been handed down over the years. But such 'management by rumours', especially when situations change rapidly, often proves to be mistaken, and is hardly the essence of the professional manager. Don't rely on biased, second-hand and misinformed reports. Get the facts.

The flow of information often needs to be improved, as it is often inadequate, and structured, to reflect changed business conditions. The situation at Burroughs Computer (now part of Unisys) appears to have been fairly typical. It was there that Michael Blumenthal, on taking control as chief executive officer, asked for regular updates on key operating statistics such as orders received, revenue and cash flow. To his surprise, however, he found that he was forced to revamp the entire accounting system to ensure that this information was available. 'You may not believe it', he said, 'but we didn't have this information in any useful way before.'

Another benefit of finding the true facts of a situation is that if people are made fully aware of the costs incurred by their actions, they will be more circumspect. Salespeople, for example, informed of the true cost of a sales call, tend to make better use of their calls and become more efficient in setting their own priorities. It is therefore important to be able to point to hard facts.

Analyzing the profitability of each product, even if with only rough estimates of relative profitability, often produces great surprise when all the costs associated with each product are included for the first time. For example, when the managing director of a certain manufacturing company decided on a 6 per cent increase in prices across the board, he wisely took the advice of his new finance director to revamp the company's accounting system to uncover the true costs of each product first. He found that two of the lines were loss-makers and could stand no price increase. They were abandoned, so preventing an estimated loss of £47,000. The prices of the remaining products were adjusted, ranging from small reductions to a 30 per cent increase. All in all, this process produced a £70,000 increase in profits above what would have been achieved if the 6 per cent across-the-board price rise had gone into effect.

Underpricing is often a symptom of lack of knowledge of true costs. This is exemplified by Bronx Engineering, an industrial equipment manufacturer which has since been acquired by another UK company. Financial control was a critical missing element in the management information system and compounded the effects of underpricing on major contracts. The resultant lack of cash prevented the company from expanding when there were plenty of orders, which had to be sub-contracted out to smaller companies. Under the resulting pressure of a £0.5 million loss on a revenue of £4 million, the company was forced to cut its workforce in half and to sell itself to another company. If the true costs of each contract had been available at an earlier stage, preferably before quoting on tenders, the company might now be thriving on its own.

Things are never quite as they might seem

It is well known that the nature of financial accounting is such that it tends to group costs in categories which may not directly reflect the operations of the company. Many industrial companies use fully absorbed manufacturing costs to set their price levels. However, when a company is unable to allocate costs adequately, this can produce a very inadequate picture of product-line profitability. An alternative approach is to value a product by its contribution margin (sales minus all variable manufacturing costs and general sales and administration expenses). This provides a more realistic profit figure on which the effect of changing prices and altering volumes can be quickly calculated. A story recounted in the *McKinsey Quarterly* [1] relates how a general manager pursued a profit opportunity based on a reinterpretation of the cost figures.

Construction materials company. The general manager of a plant in a construction materials company wanted to move up from one shift to three to get better utilization of his machinery. This would clearly require more orders and more customers. Yet the company's accountants maintained that, calculating gross margins on the basis of full manufacturing costs, the product could not be profitably transported more than 200 miles. Since the output of the plant satisfied 40 per cent of the market demand in a 200-mile radius, the general manager felt that it was unlikely that he could use price reduction to achieve further volume without causing a fierce competitive reaction.

On reviewing the figures, however, the general manager found that, by considering all the costs and benefits to the company, and using marginal costing, he could in fact deliver economically within a 700-mile radius area.

By visiting customers beyond the 200-mile radius, he discovered that by taking no more than one contract per customer per year he could win business with a 5 per cent discount in the 200–700-mile radius area without upsetting local price levels. Resultant demand was such that he was able to fill his plant for three shifts, avoid competitor retaliation, raise his contribution margin from $4 million to $9 million, and thereby triple his pre-tax profits.

The inconsistency of financial and accounting information has long been one of the prime sources of ineffective conflict and clouding of important issues in an organization. A restructuring of information systems at one well-known mail-order company was found to have considerable benefits in reducing the great amount of time that staff were previously accustomed to spending explaining the inconsistencies between the results of two different compilation methods. The employees were thus able to concentrate on the more pressing concerns which affected the company's performance.

Clearly, accurate, important and timely information presented in a usable form is one of the key elements in taking advantage of the opportunity to cut costs.

Avoid 'analysis paralysis'

A warning about the well-known 'analysis paralysis syndrome'. In difficult conditions, when problems are rapidly piling up, and decisions have to made in conditions of great uncertainty, there is always a temptation to put off decisions and wait until all the information you want appears. That day will never come. In fact, some managers spend so long analyzing their position in such enormous detail that by the time the analysis is complete the position has changed significantly.

It will always be difficult to judge whether to wait for another piece of information or to act immediately. The process should be one of gut feeling allied to common sense, with the most important facts made available in order to check that the situation is in fact as expected, and to refocus the company's efforts.

Be objective

The first step in determining cost and flexibility improvements is to start with the broadest interpretation of where the company is going. The mission statement is the objective of the journey while the strategy is the road map for getting there. Look at the sales and profits. How do they break down for each product? How have they changed over time? How have they changed relative to one another? Repeat this for costs. Only in this way will it be clear how every cost element fits into the whole picture and what its impact is on the bottom line.

It is necessary to provide definitive performance figures on business units. Setting up cost centres is a common way of ensuring that income and costs can be clearly attached to each activity. However, this is a more difficult activity for departments far from the customer, where it is hard to find the meaningful performance indicators so critical for costing and motivation. Measuring output against input, by relating to comparable activities, is the only answer.

It is a reality of business life which can often stymie an objective appraisal that cost allocations often depend more on the strength of the personality of each departmental head rather than proper strategic criteria. An objective review should look at the true facts, unencumbered by history and personalities.

Managers need to be open, honest and objective in deciding where costs and activities need to be cut. Or, as David Dworkin, the American at the head of BhS, the UK clothes store group, would have it 'there are no sacred cows' and 'there is no bullshit'.

Peeling the onion, no tears

'Peeling the onion' is a term for reviewing a company's cost position by starting from key company objectives, such as revenue, income and cash flow, and peeling back layer after layer of costs until you come to the core of the problem.

Companies have excess costs because of misallocation and inefficiency. Misallocation puts resources where they could be much better used elsewhere. This can be corrected by evaluating the contribution of each activity to the company goal.

Inefficiency is using more resources than are required. The extent to which resources can be cut can be difficult to determine – several techniques are available to do this and are presented later in this chapter in the sections dealing with best demonstrated practice and zero-based budgeting.

Take care of the pounds and the pennies will look after themselves

It makes sense to concentrate effort on the largest elements of cost because these have the greatest potential impact on the bottom line. The '80/20' rule, also known as the Pareto rule after the Italian economist of the eighteenth century who first articulated it, should be applied ruthlessly. Pareto found that it was a useful rule of thumb that, in general, 80 per cent of the contribution to any result is generated by 20 per cent of the effort expended. Therefore, it is important to focus on the key activities.

The process is that of breaking down the total cost into its biggest elements and then looking at the biggest part of that cost, and then the biggest part of that, and so on. A similar approach works well for sales and profits, as shown by Firestone.

Firestone, for instance, found that they had 7289 different varieties of tyre. Historically, they had been reluctant to discontinue product lines to avoid losing any of their customers. Nevin, the new chief executive officer, found that 65 per cent of the company's sales depended on just 25 per cent of these 7289 product variants. In consequence, he axed 2400 product categories, producing a minimal effect on sales revenue but an enormous addition to the bottom line.

Focusing also means watching your own use of time. In a chemical company, for example, a survey showed that general managers were spending less than 10 per cent of their time on key areas of their jobs.

Serving small segments where the administration costs are too high can be unprofitable and should be terminated. One of the other advantages of turning such work down is that competitors pick up the business to the detriment of their own profitability.

The Helena Rubinstein cosmetics company is often held up as an example of a lack of focus causing a company's downfall, and later the use of focus to revive it.

Helena Rubinstein, the cosmetics company, was acquired by Colgate Palmolive in 1973 for $142 million. In 1978 it was losing money and by 1979 Colgate was looking for a buyer. It was not until July 1980 that Helena Rubinstein was sold, to Albi Enterprises for $20 million on a down-payment of just $1.5 million with the rest payable over the next 15 years, with Colgate guaranteeing $43 million of bank debt. It was clear that there was a 'lot of pressure on Colgate to sell'.

Albi managed to turn the company around by focusing on the biggest potential profit generators for the company. Five or six countries accounted for 90 per cent of sales, and in many markets the Helena Rubinstein operation was performing reasonably well. While the US, England and Japan, representing 38 per cent of sales, were in real trouble, it was found that the 'franchise was still magnificent at customer level'.

Colgate had always emphasized volume and was reluctant to cut back any operations. However, Albi sold the mass-market operations which were inconsistent with the upmarket Helena Rubinstein image. Concentrating on profitable and expanding lines only, half the sales-force was cut. Plants around the world were shut down and manufacturing was centred on the European plant.

By focusing on the most profitable lines, Albi was able to buy the company cheaply and quickly, fix it swiftly and make money. As Al Burak, the then president of Helena Rubinstein, once said, 'You can make big money buying trouble'.

Companies must apply the basic expedients of getting the facts and concentrating on the areas with greatest impact on the bottom line. The case of the British manufacturing industry shows that it is not focusing its efforts on what might seem clear imperatives. A recent report attacked the sector's tendency to focus on reducing direct labour costs when overheads and materials account for by far the biggest proportion of factory costs. Another study showed that for a typical engineering company, one of the biggest single charges against profits was financing costs. Hence, a key aspect to consider is minimizing working capital.

Perhaps Sir John Harvey-Jones sums up the strategy most succinctly. You have to be 'absolutely clear what is the key part of the business, the bit you want to grow, as this is the bit you want to come out stronger. You must look to reinforce this in a recession and cut the other bits more. Managers don't do this. They cop out.'

The boiled frog syndrome

You may have heard of the remarkable behaviour of a certain frog which, if dropped into boiling water, will immediately spring out, yet when placed into a pot of cold water which is slowly heated will remain in the water and gradually succumb as it boils.

What, you're thinking, has this to do with managers? Well, many managers, being in the thick of things, are often unable to detect gradual yet important changes until it is too late. Critically important to managers are changes which raise the importance of previously inconsequential items to critically significant status. That is the relevance of the boiled frog syndrome. Or, in other words, small changes can have big effects over time.

Cost structures, for example, can change significantly over time. There may be an important reason for their growing so fast, and the consequences can be significant. For example, it is instructive to look back at the change in the relative cost positions for Japanese and American cars sold in the US between 1956 and 1976. During those 20 years the cost leadership position of the US was entirely reversed, mainly due to Japan's relatively faster growing wage productivity. This has allowed the Japanese to land superior quality cars at lower prices. One serious effect has been the great loss of market share by the domestic producers. However, the US auto industry has been responding by cutting costs using automation and out-sourcing of components, slimming down of workforces, better inventory management and faster model turnaround.

Another illustration is provided by the steel industry in the US which has been shaken up by a new form of mill, the 'minimill' (see page 123). US Steel (now USX), the largest US integrated steel producer, realizing it could never compete successfully with the minimills, which used new economies to achieve lower costs, chose to exit from the rod, light wire and structurals market rather than continue to sell the entire range of steel products.

Talk to your people

It is surprisingly rare to find companies soliciting their people for their opinions on how to cut costs. Yet when a company is clear about its aims and communicates them openly to its workforce, and asks for their help, treating their opinions with respect, the results can be truly phenomenal. Ford illustrates this well.

Ford Taurus. For its Taurus (Granada) programme, Ford made a point of spending a great deal of time talking to its hourly paid 'blue collar' workers, asking them how it could make the model easier to build. Out of this process came some 1400 suggestions, of which 550 were incorporated in the final design. 'It's amazing', declared a manufacturing engineer, 'the dedication and commitment you can get from people. We will never go back to the old way because we know so much of what they can bring to the party.' Talking to the workforce was just one of the innovations that led Ford to report 1989 profits which exceeded those of General Motors, its principal rival, for the first time.

Another way of eliciting good ideas from the workforce is through suggestion schemes. Such schemes have to be actively managed but the rewards for the organization can be considerable. BTR's Dunlop subsidiary, for example, gained a total saving of £54,000 in one year. The potential is highlighted by research carried out in 1988 by the UK's Industrial Society. It showed that, for the 103 companies identified, one in five workers on average had sent in a suggestion. That 22 per cent of the suggestions were implemented demonstrates the quality of entries.

The Industrial Society recommends several key factors for maximizing the value of a suggestions scheme.

- Management support and resources must be allocated to it: some companies fund brainstorming sessions once a month in a local pub.
- They should be actively promoted to the workforce using the company magazine and announcing winners.
- They should be fun.
- Suggestions must be handled quickly and efficiently so that employees do not lose enthusiasm.
- Submitting an idea should be rewarded: schemes surveyed by the Industrial Society paid an average of 18 per cent of the annual savings; other companies reward with £5 minimum for every entry.

Suggestions schemes are only successful when management recognizes their potential and supports them.

Setting targets

There are two important techniques which are of real importance in setting targets: best demonstrated practice and zero-based budgeting. Both of these techniques are extremely useful in discovering the extent of misallocation and waste.

Best demonstrated practice

The best demonstrated practice (BDP) technique helps managers by providing some basis of comparison against which to judge the efficiency of a unit. By finding comparable figures for efficiency, a comparison provides a target to aim for. Then the challenge 'if they can do it, so can we' can be sent out.

BDP is particularly useful for dealing with indirect costs. In most companies, indirect costs represent a significant proportion of total costs. Unfortunately, it is very difficult to measure waste and inefficiency for indirect costs, thereby making the consideration of efficiency an haphazard affair. The difficulty is finding relevant, meaningful, easily calculated and comparable output figures to compare with input figures.

The main options are comparing performance for a given business unit over time, against similar departments or plants in the company, against competitors, or against similar departments in other non-competing companies. Each option is now dealt with in turn.

BDP against time

Over the years of a boom period, it is inevitable that a great deal of waste will have been built up. The amount of wastage can be determined by comparing historical figures with current figures.

By looking for the time when the cost of a function was lowest, then putting the manager of that function on the spot by asking him why he can't get back to that figure (adjusting for external events such as sales growth, margin strategy, etc), the manager can be inspired and pressured to find ways of approaching his previous efficiency performance.

Managers should be asking themselves why the figures have changed, or why they haven't changed more. What is the main driver of the costs (number of orders, size of orders, relative size of customers, etc)? Could some of the changes be related to the main driver? Could they represent inefficiency creeping in? Could more have been done? Has a previous efficiency drive stalled? British Airways, for example, employed approximately 250 staff per aircraft over a decade ago. Despite extensive efficiency drives, this figure is still 200 per aircraft. Yet some comparable competitors have managed to achieve 50 staff per aircraft.

BDP across comparable business units

This approach can be most instructive. Some of the questions which could be asked include, 'Is there a reason why one plant is more efficient than another?' Or, more specifically, 'Why is it that the ratio of one section's fixed costs to its revenue are much higher than that of a comparable business unit?' US Steel and Stone-Platt illustrate the value of this approach.

US Steel. A US steel company with four separate steel-making plants compared the cost structures of each of these plants. They reasoned that each plant would be better than the others in at least one major way. Therefore, if each of the best productivity standards could be incorporated in all plants, then each would be more efficient than the very best plant. One of the many valuable results was that over $200 million of annual energy cost-saving potential was identified throughout the four plants.

Stone-Platt acquired an American firm making similar products and was surprised to find that the US company, with one-third of the workforce, was making twice the sales and value-added per man as in the UK. After carefully analyzing and discounting the influences of equivalent equipment, a more standardized product, a more pronounced work ethic and a bigger home market, the reason for the astonishingly higher productivity was isolated as the Americans' design of the product for manufacture. The UK company therefore invested a great deal of effort in improving the design for manufacture of the British product.

Using competitors as best demonstrated practice

One of the most useful ways of setting a level of expenditure is to compare the company with competitors. The best competitor may then become the best demonstrated practice. This is sometimes known as 'benchmarking'. Indeed, the Japanese are known to use the performance of their competitors as 'the goal'. A good application of the approach is that of determining the relative cost position (RCP), as the following example shows.

German vs British factory. A study on overmanning reported in one of the UK's leading management journals, *Management Today* [2], compared workforce levels of a British factory against a German factory producing closely similar products. Comparing like with like, it was found that the German factory had 39 per cent less people in their factory for the same output. Further analysis provided a percentage breakdown of the causes of this discrepancy:

Plant layout	20 per cent
Mechanization	27 per cent
Versatility of skills	10 per cent
Cultural and social	9 per cent
Other	20 per cent
Residual (unknown)	14 per cent
	100 per cent

This provided objectives for the British factory to aim for.

In times of plenty it is possible for quality to be achieved through the very expensive method of overchecking and the toleration of high rework levels. This was the problem faced by Jaguar on privatization. But just where should the line be drawn?

Jaguar. By comparing its performance with that of its competitors, Jaguar felt that having 12 per cent of its workforce inspecting its product was excessive and so disbanded half of its inspection teams, forcing the company to find more cost-effective means of ensuring high quality.

Jaguar sent senior managers to visit its arch rivals BMW, Mercedes-Benz and various firms in Japan to learn their management and quality control techniques. This resulted in the introduction of informal quality circles and a successful suggestions scheme.

Avoiding the 'not invented here' syndrome

Every competitor can teach even the best companies something useful. As Emerson once said: 'Every man I meet is my superior in some way. In that, I learn of him.' The insidious arrogance of the 'not-invented-here' syndrome is well known as being a major factor in preventing best intentions from being realized. When Volkswagen's innovative car, the Beetle, for instance, was brought to England after the Second World War and UK motor manufacturers were invited to view it in order to adopt some of its many innovations, they are reported to have treated it with disdain. Yet many of its Porsche design features are used in cars today, and that model sold many millions throughout the world.

Understanding the costs of a competing product can point out real opportunities and real threats. Looking at products in the way a customer might, for example, is a useful way of bringing these to light. Products and services which can be made to substitute for others at a cheaper price are good examples of opportunities to cut costs. Higher steel prices, for example, mainly due to a sharp rise in oil prices, caused masonry buildings to be more cost effective than steel-framed buildings in 1974. This represented an opportunity for constructors of masonry buildings. Similarly, in the early 1980s, many companies found that they faced an entirely different set of customers as their product range moved from mechanical to predominantly electronic technology. This represented an opportunity for forward-looking firms.

The decade of 'know your customer' may, according to industry observers, have changed to a 'know your competitor' strategy now that conditions are difficult and competition is fierce. One of the most important factors in the success of such an attitude is the change in orientation from absolute to relative achievement. You now have something to compare with, something to aim to beat, as ABB has learnt.

ABB. Formed by the merger of Sweden's ASEA and Switzerland's Brown Boveri in 1987, ABB is one of the world's strongest electrical engineering groups. Percy Barnevik, president and chief executive, has turned performance around but feels he has some way to go. 'Now the problem is that they get so happy when they see profits doubled; they think 4 per cent [margin] is fantastic; and you have to tell them that American competitors can make 10 per cent.'

Determining competitors' cost positions can require some effort. It is rarely possible to determine exact figures, and so 'soft' data has to be accepted. This type of data is produced by taking publicly available accounts and adding in information from other sources: newspaper and trade magazine articles, conversations with trade organization representatives, chats with rivals at exhibitions, data from new employees who have come from those companies, or even from top-level discussions with their directors. Where gaps remain, equivalent figures from within your company are used and then adjusted as required for the rival's conditions. The following example illustrates how this technique was used by Ford.

Ford strips down competitor products, then reverse-engineers them to calculate their costs. Then the economies of scale can be calculated, knowing the number of people employed and the number of cars produced over a certain period. The competitors' break-even points can be determined, since Ford is able to substitute its own figures for any gaps. From this process, Ford was able to show that the BMC (later British Leyland) Mini was not making any money for some time after its launch in August 1959, and subsequently decided not to enter the UK small car market while the price remained so low.

The presence of objective standards of performance on which to base action plans is critical. As we have seen, much higher productivity levels and lower costs allowed Japanese auto producers to land models in the US costing $1500–2000 less than they could be made for in Detroit. General Motors, Ford and Chrysler used this essential information as the basis for their performance objectives.

BDP of comparable functions in non-competitors

Another useful way in which companies can use BDP is to compare performance of the same activity across non-competing companies, even in entirely different fields of business.

General Electric. Jack Welch, the chief executive officer of General Electric (GE) in the US, has pushed a global best practices programme through his company. GE has visited Ford for ideas on product development and employee involvement. Digital Equipment Corporation helps with asset management and American Express with customer satisfaction. Hewlett-Packard provides suggestions on partnerships with suppliers and quality improvement. GE has also gone to Honda for ideas on managing the product development process.

Once the data has been collected and compared, the questioning of why some figures and percentages are higher begins – and what has to be done to get them down. There should be no illusions. Such benchmarking is easy in theory but tough in practice. But the BDP method does represent one of the few rational ways by which to measure and reduce inefficiency where absolute efficiency measures do not exist.

Zero-based budgeting

There is a need for organizations to change in accordance with market and technical changes, but it is difficult to find objective comparisons for truly unique organizations. Triangulating with the BDP method and other techniques already mentioned is the zero-based budgeting (ZBB) method.

A typical use of ZBB is to request each unit manager to propose a quantity of resources for his area of responsibility and to justify every pound in that proposal by demonstrating the benefit of his unit to the company. That is, he starts from scratch, or 'ground zero', and builds up the organization on paper to what it should be in its perfect form.

Instead of just being seen as a cost-cutting technique, ZBB can also be a powerful tool in improving competitive advantage. For example, if a manager could demonstrate the value of a trade-off between minimal funding, service levels and customer satisfaction compared to competitors, he could legitimately be allocated more funds.

National Power. A good illustration of the practical use of the ZBB technique is that of National Power, the UK power-generating company, which announced a 50 per cent cut in its 'white collar' staff. Much of this was justified by a ZBB exercise.

A team of four staff invented a brand-new corporation, dubbed 'Notional Power', which was designed to meet the demands of National Power's customers. They asked themselves what would be the minimum overhead necessary for a company with the same assets as National Power to run its business. By contracting out design, devolving procurement to the stations themselves, and by improving efficiencies in maintenance of buildings, Notional Power ended up with less than half the number of white collar employees of the National Power organization. Combined with competitor comparison, 2000 jobs were cut, saving several hundreds of millions of pounds over a three- to four-year period.

Perhaps a simpler but equally useful approach is to use the ZBB philosophy to ask yourself, 'Do we really need activity X?' In this way, ZBB is a useful way of eliminating waste. One manufacturing company, for example, had a team of 18 working on rewriting the standards by which operations were to be carried out. It was discovered that they were mainly rewriting existing European standards and that there was little difference. The entire team was therefore closed down with no apparent detriment to the firm with the personnel allocated to other departments.

ZBB can be a very rigorous way of setting targets and should be seen as defining the limits of the possible. The managing director of one company used ZBB in just such an extreme fashion. By preparing pessimistic sales forecasts and defining the profit desired, then removing direct costs, the gap that was left had to make do for overheads. This sum was then divided across divisions by priority. Those units for which no money had been allocated were forced to close. In this way the company was able to reduce its indirect workforce by one-third.

Targets must, of course, be realistic and the ease of reduction of each cost centre needs to be factored in. Time and resources are needed to achieve these targets – they can't be achieved overnight and will need continual high-level prodding.

Making the cuts

Eliminate waste quickly

'Success breeds success' is a well-known saying. In the context of cost-cutting, this means going for those 'quick wins' which rapidly produce results.

BhS. Simply by 'tweaking' and removing inefficiency quickly, soon after his arrival in November 1989, David Dworkin brought quick cost savings to BhS, a leading UK clothing retailer and a subsidiary of the Storehouse Group. As chief executive, he reduced the amount of merchandise sitting in stock rooms and set fallow footage to work. Dworkin told American shareholders that he was horrified to find four-year-old stock in his stores. He was even more alarmed when some of the stores claimed that they could not take in new stock because there was no room for it.

Restructuring costs, significant buying and marketing personnel changes, 10 per cent mark-downs to shift obsolete stock and deeper than expected problems at BhS have delayed its enduring turnaround. However, the immediate effects of the cost-cutting drive were that BhS trebled its operating profits in the first half of 1990.

The extent of waste in companies is often surprising. In his autobiography, Marcus Sieff of the UK clothing and food retailer Marks & Spencer, relates the result of 'Operation Simplification', carried out when he was chairman.

'It's time we checked which of our systems are no longer necessary and what we really need', Simon Marks, son of one of the founders, remarked to him. After some six months' patient study it was found that the so-called 'pink slip', a stock transfer document issued in triplicate, was superfluous. Its elimination led to the removal of 26 million pieces of paper and over a thousand filing cabinets from the system. The annual cost savings in time and effort are probably incalculable.

Communication of targets

Making clear the goals of each company unit and its performance in meeting those targets, such as displaying them openly to workers on boards, as is found in Japanese companies, will often produce results as employees motivate themselves to narrow the difference.

Rationalizing is hard to do

> **Wadkin** machine tools, one of the brightest jewels in the UK industry for wood-working equipment, dropped about a third of its range, augmenting its own products by distributing some imported Italian machines. The company found this a good way of reducing costs while maintaining sales. As Goddard, the chief executive, explains: 'It's a hard thing to rationalize in a recession – most people do the opposite.'

There are many anecdotes about product rationalization but I particularly like the story of a household goods company which merged with another company in order to bring a new product line into its range. In one of the early post-merger meetings the management was asked to bring along a sample of each package of each variety of the product. The conference room, it was related, was so overflowing with packages that the meeting almost had to be held in another room.

This is a case where the much overlooked 'cost of complexity' rears its head. This is the indirect cost of having many product varieties where each additional product requires significant extra administrative costs. Cost of complexity is often overlooked by managers because it is difficult to quantify. An example of one organization which has been able to expose this cost is Britain's National Health Service (NHS). Consultants working closely with the NHS have managed to show that the addition to its enormous product range of just one product, such as an alternative type of surgical glove, adds between £500 and £1000 a year to operating overheads. The NHS has begun to respond by carefully evaluating the need for so many variants and standardizing where possible.

Use your buying power

Recessions provide good opportunities to exact cost benefits from suppliers by using the company's buying power. This is possible when a seller is more dependent on a buyer than a buyer is on a seller.

To possess buying power a company needs to be able to take a large share of its suppliers' output and either threaten to go to alternative suppliers or to produce in-house. Rationalizing your list of suppliers can often become a way of increasing your buying power.

Buying power is an opportunity to win concessions which are not based on cost savings to the supplier. This would include trade rebates, cumulative volume discounts or more frequent deliveries. Large building contractors, for example, with good order books negotiated at the end of the previous boom at top-of-the-cycle prices have found that they can improve their margins by squeezing the subcontractors who were short of work at that time.

Practice makes perfect

Substantial cost reductions can come from learning how to do the job more efficiently with practice. Literally hundreds of studies have shown that costs usually decline by 10 to 30 per cent with each doubling of cumulated output. In other words, activities follow 'experience curves' which fall in the 70 to 90 per cent range. For example, a well-managed plant producing a constant output of limestone powder from rock has been found to have the potential for a 20 per cent reduction in costs as the total number of tonnes produced over time doubles. The best explanation of the experience curve effect is that the company and its employees are learning how to do things more efficiently. In a plant producing a constant output, this is a matter of time. If the plant has varying output, then the best measure of experience is the cumulative number of output produced. Of course, it must be emphasized that the experience curve effects represent potential savings only. These cost reductions have to be deliberately managed and worked at.

Perhaps the best-known early user of the experience curve principle is Henry Ford.

Ford. By using new techniques, improved over time, Ford made the whole experience curve concept an integral part of his strategy. By cutting the price of his product, he attracted vast increases in demand as the market opened up to those who could then afford a car. As he made more and more units, so the organization improved the way it made the 'Tin Lizzies', and so the cost dropped further. In this way, Ford was able to increase profits as the price was reduced. Looking at the figures for the Model T will show this more dramatically. In 1910, Ford produced 12,000 cars at a price of $950. By 1926, he had made a total of 15 million cars and they were selling for $270. Allowing for inflation during those 16 years, the $950 price had fallen to $200 in 1910 dollars. Hence, Ford had managed to bring down the cost per unit by 14 per cent every time the number of cars had doubled. In other words, the experience curve had a slope of 86 per cent. By 1927, however, Ford's strategy of one model 'in any colour you want so long as it's black' was circumvented by General Motors, which offered a wider range, but at a price premium. Ford was forced to close his entire plant for a year for a model change.

Costs may be shared across several products and then further cut by use of the experience curve principle. Consider an electrical consumer durables company which makes three products: an electric pencil sharpener, a small desktop fan and a portable drill. The motor, common to all three, is made in-house, and represents about 30 per cent of the total manufactured costs. By standardizing the motor, the cumulative volume of a single model will increase much faster than if three separate motors were manufactured.

Interestingly, one of the reasons why Japanese motorcycle companies were able to decimate the British motorcycle industry was the use of the experience curve effect. When the Japanese first landed small motorcycles in the UK, the domestic companies moved into niches of bigger and more powerful models, where they felt safe. But the Japanese defined their industry more broadly than the British to take into account the interrelated experience, and therefore shared costs, of making small and large motorcycles. Hence, they were able to make large motorcycles in volume at an acceptable profit margin, causing the domestic competitors to exit the market for good.

Analyzing the cost per unit (in inflation-adjusted terms) against cumulative output can help in setting targets. Here, you need to ask whether demand is sufficiently stable to justify an experience curve strategy, and whether cumulative output is doubling fast enough for the experience curve to provide any strategic advantage. In addition, success with the experience curve depends on whether the company can keep its cost reductions proprietary. Japanese motor manufacturers, for example, deliberately design their own machine tools in order to produce machine tools better suited to their needs, and in so doing their innovations remain secret.

Increasing costs to decrease costs

This, at first sight paradoxical, approach has served several companies well, as now shown.

> **Electrical Group**. A London-based subsidiary of a major electrical group was paying its personnel at its London plant the same low wages as at its Tyneside plant. Since the salary levels in London are generally higher than elsewhere, this led to the calibre of the staff in London being low. Absenteeism and overtime were excessive, with extraordinarily high scrap levels of 20 per cent. It proved impractical to transfer people from one plant to the other, or to transfer the work to the Tyneside plant. The solution adopted by top management was to offer 20 per cent higher wages in London to attract the right sort of workers. The result was that productivity increased by over 25 per cent and £60,000 was saved on reduced scrap levels. The firm was also able to close its Tyneside factory, freeing £600,000 in working capital. Hence, increasing costs can decrease costs.
>
> **BOC**. 'We deliberately chose to invest in a recession', explained Richard Giordano, boss of BOC, the international air products group. BOC's capital expenditure was reported to have risen almost four-fold in as many years through the recessionary years of the early 1980s. One of the results was that the cost levels of a new plant at Charleston became half that of the older plants. 'I wish we'd done it years ago', says Giordano.

So, even in a cost-cutting exercise, there will be areas where it may well be justified to increase costs in order to decrease the total costs.

Investing for the future

When cutting costs, you need to think hard about your priorities. The purpose of this section is to show you how to avoid short-sightedness creeping into the cost-reduction process: he who only thinks of the present has no future. (Maintaining advertising is covered in more detail in Chapter 8.)

Maintaining research and development

For many businesses it is important to continue to invest in research and development (R&D) because of the long lead time of the process. Cincinnatti Milacron, for instance, is a leading US machine-tool maker under severe pressure from Japanese competitors. In order to survive when many of its domestic competitors have ceased to exist it has had to adopt a policy of pushing ahead with new R&D programmes regardless of the business cycle. In a market with shortening product life cycles, a delay of a year or more would cripple its long-term success.

J C Bamford (JCB) Excavators is a UK success story and a firm also under pressure from the Japanese. A small company, it is the global market leader in the manufacture of so-called backhoe loaders – twin-ended, earth-moving machines with a shovel at the front end and an excavator arm at the rear. Competing head-on with the likes of Komatsu and Caterpillar, it struggled to flourish when its market plummeted 40 per cent in ten years and discounting became rife. JCB's solution was to cut costs and to invest in strategically important technology, even in the middle of the recession. A £7 million investment in what was described by *Advanced Manufacturing Technology* magazine as 'Britain's first computer-controlled manufacturing plant for engineering products' has borne fruit with an increased market share after coming on-line in 1986 for the return of the boom times. Product groups consisting of several departments working together during the downturn have led to the emergence of new products with a greater sensitivity to customers' needs.

Dow Chemical recognizes that R&D is not an activity which can be turned on and off like a tap. In a year of heavy losses for the European chemical industry, Dow Chemical continued to pour into Europe almost 10 per cent of its annual revenue in the form of investment and R&D, and at a time when its operating income declined by over a half to just $135 million. 'The winners will be the companies that keep costs under control and grab the growth markets', declared the president of Dow Europe.

Maintaining investment

Other forms of investment provide long-term benefits which require preparation before they are realized. Wadkin and Renault provide two contrasting examples.

Wadkin, the leader in UK wood-working tools, invested some £2 million in 20 machine tools and essential computer systems which were ordered and commissioned in the very depths of the recession in the 18 months to the end of 1981. Such a high-risk policy of investing in product innovation and machinery had its pay-off in providing much increased profits and maintaining a 50 per cent share of the UK wood-working machinery market.

Renault, the French automobile manufacturer, provides an example of a company that failed to prepare for the future. Along with its rival PSA (Peugeot) in the French market, it had postponed painful retrenchment and was then faced with an industry overcapacity of 20 per cent. In addition, Renault, having failed to anticipate the shortening of product life cycles, came under severe pricing pressure due to its lack of competitive new models. Renault then had to rely on discounting to compete. Its market share fell in a few short years from 40 to 31 per cent. In one year, while the market fell 13 per cent, Renault suffered the indignity of a 23 per cent fall in demand. A resultant record loss of over £1 billion was the legacy of failing to keep up its new product development.

Renault will have to improve even further to keep up with its competition: Peugeot aims to reduce the time between initial design and commercial production from the present five years to four. Furthermore, the French market is likely to be opened up to the Japanese competition in the near future.

Maintaining training

Many companies abandon their training plans in a downturn and do not take on board new people. With the passage of time, this can result in deficiencies in companies' skill requirements, especially when the implications of adverse demographics in much of the Western world are considered.

In this chapter, we have discussed the many opportunities that companies have open to them in difficult times to cut costs. Firms emerge leaner than before and, by saving resources, can take advantage of the opportunity presented by the downturn itself, and exploit the benefits through the upswing and into the following boom period.

Chapter 5 deals with improving the flexibility of the company.

Chapter 5

Improving Flexibility

Flexibility is the key

All forecasts understate inherent uncertainty, so companies need to be flexible. Downturns provide many opportunities for a slimmed-down flexible company which is nimble enough to take advantage of these opportunities better than the competition.

Flexibility means fast decision-making and having costs as variable and low as is strategically viable. It is critical that the decision structure is not bloated; its prevention leads to flexibility through people. In swiftly changing times, flexibility of corporate mind and body are essential.

It was the great military strategist Clausewitz who declared that three-quarters of all decisions are made in the face of great uncertainty. Company strategy therefore needs to be flexible to take advantage of shifting markets and environments. A favourite example of management writer Peter Drucker which illustrates this is the comparison of the two American department store chains Sears and its rival Montgomery Ward. Immediately following the Second World War, Montgomery Ward, relying on expert forecasts which predicted a recession, prepared for a sales decline. Sears, instead, followed its own store traffic and saw no slacking off in revenue. Sears then decided to expand. As a result, Sears captured the number one retailing position which was unthreatened for 30 years.

Making costs as variable as possible

Bringing down the break-even point

Being able to produce more profits from a smaller volume of work means a lower break-even point. The break-even volume, the minimum demand required for the organization not to make a loss, is defined by the level of the company's fixed costs, variable costs and price per unit.

Cutting fixed costs is one of the most common strategies for bringing down the break-even point. US Steel (now USX), for instance, brought down its break-even point from over 80 per cent of capacity to under 70 per cent in less than two years, mainly by reducing its number of blast furnaces from 43 to 25 and improving their productivity. For an organization with such enormous fixed assets, this process provided an improved ability to maintain profits as demand for its products fell.

Some companies bring their fixed costs down but leave themselves flexible by moth-balling temporarily. Shipowners, for example, moor their ships in a shutdown state with a skeleton maintenance crew. The fixed cost of their crews and fuel is vastly reduced and the shipowners can avoid taking a great loss from having to sell the ships at the bottom of the market when there is a glut of ships. Yet the ships are still available to be brought into action at relatively short notice.

Some cardboard drum manufacturers rely on a similar strategy for their existence. In boom times, they use highly depreciated machinery and temporary unskilled staff. When the market falls and the resultant overcapacity makes production uneconomic, they shut up shop for a year or more until the industry depression is over. Then they re-emerge from their hibernation into the sunlight.

Another way of reducing break-even points is by increasing the proportion of variable to fixed costs; that is, making fixed costs variable. This has a similar effect on improving the break-even position as cutting fixed costs. In addition, this strategy has the advantage of leading to faster growth of profits in the upturn.

Service companies tend to have low investment ratios. For a manufacturing company, an increase in the degree of subcontracting of non-core activities can be a route to bringing down the fixed:variable cost ratio.

Delegate, don't dissipate

Successful companies concentrate on doing what they are best at, and what they earn the greatest profit at. In this way, they are not held back by the need for investment and management time for lesser contributing activities. Companies should look at doing what they are good at, and find other people to do what's left.

A good illustration of this principle is provided by the example of the lawyer and his secretary. The lawyer was making $200,000 but found he was spending half of his time on administration. He realized that what he really enjoyed, what he was of course valued for, was his legal acumen, not his administrative skills. While he felt that, with his specific knowledge, he could do a better job than any secretary, he decided to hire a secretary at a salary of $30,000 on a short-term basis. By doing this, he could double the amount of time spent on clients, nearly double his income and avoid the loathsome part of the business. The lawyer had learned not to dissipate his energies but to delegate. Another important lesson that the anecdote teaches is that the ability to delegate often depends on being able to accept second best. In the same way, companies should investigate the use of management time and effort on non-core activities and see whether some activities can be better done outside the company.

Disintegration

There has been many a pitched battle fought on the field of management between the land of vertical integration and the country of flexibility. Vertical integration, or controlling the activities upstream and/or downstream of a product, is often seen as attractive because it allows more control and can cut out an intermediary, leading to the 'repatriation' of those profits. But in a downturn, not all of the capacity can always be used, leading to excess costs in-house.

One way out, at least in part, as some companies have found, is always to have some slack capacity allocated to external customers. In this way, contracts have already been established before the downturn, when preferred supplier status will help in finding more capacity-filling work.

The argument can lean towards the flexibility of sourcing supplies outside. Every company has to examine where its unique selling proposition (USP) lies: what does it provide that is truly unique among its competitors?

Farming out activities to outside contractors can have real advantages. There are often accompanying reductions in overall cost caused, for example, by the more motivated and potentially more efficient entrepreneurial firm doing your payroll, or effected by utilizing the specialized skills and capacity of an outside firm. Subcontracting can also provide the benefits of not tying up so much cash, and therefore can produce a higher return on capital employed.

This is the basis on which Electronic Data Systems (EDS), which has a $6 billion turnover, has based its remarkable rise to number one in the US $40 billion market for information technology services. The founder, Ross Perot, discovered that he could save its 700 customers money by running their computer networks on contract more cheaply that they could. EDS makes its money by utilizing its economies of scale in buying customers' equipment and new equipment, and in running the systems. Combined with its ability to keep up with the industry's technical advances – beyond the scope of most customers – EDS owns its niche by providing real customer benefits, allowing them to save money and concentrate on their prime activities.

General Motors, traditionally a highly integrated company, reacted to the oil crisis of the 1970s by reorganizing to cope with the competition of imports from Japan. It reduced its vertical integration by shopping for lower-cost components worldwide. It reduced its horizontal integration – that is, making a wide range of products – by badge-engineering products made by other companies, such as Isuzu of Japan.

On a smaller scale, there is the example of a certain furniture company.

Furniture company. A furniture company using its own transport to deliver weekly to a number of regional depots found that using an outside contractor made better sense. The specialist transport firm was able to guarantee delivery within 24 hours to any customer in the UK – better than the average performance achieved by the branches. The furniture company therefore closed its regional depots and sold its vehicles to the contractor. The company released £630,000 in cost savings and working capital.

Balancing reduction of fixed costs against strategic goals

It is important not to eliminate those fixed costs which are required to meet the company's strategic goals. The oil company Exxon, for example, made a 28 per cent cut in workforce in 1986 at the time of an oil price cut. Since then Exxon has suffered a rash of safety and leak incidents, such as the *Exxon Valdez* spillage in Alaska and the Bayway, New Jersey leak. The *Wall Street Journal* speculated on a connection between these incidents and the cut in workforce.

The running-aground of the *Valdez* in early 1989, spilling 11 million gallons of oil and contaminating over 1000 miles of coastline, has cost the company in excess of $2 billion. Repairing its negative public image has been an additional major expense and has done the company's reputation considerable harm. It is clearly necessary for companies to examine the wider impact of cutting fixed costs.

Cost reduction can damage the company's competitive advantage in many other ways if not done with care. General management should make itself aware of critical cost-cutting decisions, and lower-level managers should understand the company's mission. In that way, they can make informed decisions.

Service levels offered to customers is an example which springs instantly to mind to illustrate this point. Imagine that a controller of inventory decides to cut inventory in order to reduce carrying costs. But if the company's main competitive advantage and selling point is the ability to supply instantly from stock, he and general management may be working at cross-purposes. The inventory controller and general management need to get together to agree on levels which meet both their requirements in the best interests of the company.

Underpaid service workers have long been a major management problem in the US. Low levels of motivation, job dissatisfaction, high staff turnover and, ultimately, dissatisfied customers can too easily result in such an environment. False economies can defeat the intent of even the most extensive cost-cutting programme. Many companies are now paying more attention to such trade-offs and there is evidence of some companies increasing their personnel budgets to reduce such undesirable side-effects.

Increasing flexibility through people

'Excessive organizational structure is the principal cause of slow corporate response to changed circumstances', wrote Tom Peters, author of the best-selling *In Search of Excellence*. Taking advantage of the opportunities in a downturn requires flexibility to cope with hard-to-predict changes. This means cutting dead wood from the decision structure and making the whole organization more flexible in its outlook.

Using the opportunity to cut labour costs

A labour cost advantage negotiated in the pit of a recession can be managed intelligently so that it remains in place throughout the next cycle, where the true benefits can be reaped. This important opportunity provided by a downturn was exploited by International Harvester (as it was known in the early 1980s) where McCardell, the new chief executive officer, recognized that he had inherited a bloated cost structure. This had been caused by the company having bought industrial peace for the last 20 years by excessive wage increases not linked to productivity. McCardell was able to use the serious crisis the company was in to dismantle and restructure the labour cost structure.

Cutting labour costs means improving productivity, cutting the workforce, or reducing the wage levels. The deregulated US airline industry of the early 1980s is a good example of possible approaches. Faced with much increased competition, some forced down labour costs (like Continental and American), others maintained a flexible workforce (like Delta and Southwest), while others structured their operations (like People Express and Pan-Am) to avoid the overhead problems of the traditional carriers.

However, crying wolf by repeatedly raising the spectre of crises can be counter-productive, as found by Frank Borman, the ex-astronaut and chief executive officer of the now-bankrupt Eastern Airlines, in the early 1980s. He faced a credibility gap as a result of workers' familiarity with gloomy predictions. He conceded that: 'We've had a weakness in bringing the truth to the employees in a manner that was believable.'

More flexibility through the better use of people

Wage concessions may well evaporate during the upturn after a recession if not very carefully managed. Even worse, they may lead to strikes or labour disruption. Consequently, permanent improvements in productivity, such as flexible skilling and team working, can be more useful to a company than cutting wages and salaries. Employees stand to benefit as well, as exemplified by Caterpillar, which was engaged in a wage-round battle with the United Auto Workers union in a serious industry downturn. Instead of agreeing on a 3 per cent annual wage increase, the union was persuaded to adopt a productivity-building, profit-sharing plan.

Productivity improvements are also easier to 'sell' to the workforce than wage cuts since they can help to reduce or prevent lay-offs. These concessions are extremely difficult to gain at any time other than in a crisis like a recession. The scale of the opportunity is exemplified by Toshiba's overhaul of a UK factory and the varied examples which follow.

Toshiba. When, in a deep economic recession, Toshiba took over the television factory in Plymouth, England, which it had previously run in a joint venture, it was forced to reduce effective labour costs significantly. The threat to survival provided the spur to workers' flexibility initiatives and the introduction of single-union bargaining. Union official Ron Pemberton described the feelings of the workforce. 'The shock of being out of work was very great. If they turned to you and asked if you would accept flexibility or whatever, there were ten people in the queue behind you who would, so you said yes. They could practically put in any conditions they wanted.'

City of St Louis. Some years ago, the city of St Louis was faced with a severe regional recession. In an effort to solve the problems, companies and workers got together to form the St Louis PRIDE labour-management agreements. Rigid job demarcation was eliminated and the right of management to manage acknowledged. A union official agreed that it was unlikely that this could have occurred at any other time.

Toyota's high productivity owes its existence to the introduction, during difficult times, of the company's much vaunted *kanban* or just-in-time method of manufacturing. It was Toyota's near-bankruptcy in the depths of a working capital crisis early in its existence which led it to introduce the technique in order to free up vital working capital. Toyota is now a highly successful global company and the *kanban* method is a much-studied technique.

IBM. In a recent period of industry overcapacity and stagnant demand, IBM moved staff into front-line roles in order to improve returns per employee and to avoid lay-offs. At IBM Germany, the president, Hans-Olaf Henkel, reported that the number of employees with direct contact with customers, as opposed to administrative jobs, has risen by 40 per cent in the last three years of the 1990s, with only a slight rise in employees.

All offices, as many an experienced manager knows, look busy. The only way to measure performance is to compare output with input. Low productivity is sometimes an intentional by-product of workers wanting to build up their more lucrative overtime earnings. One company's solution to this was to cancel all overtime and to pay everyone their previous average earnings with a reduction of working hours from 47 to 40 hours per week. The result was a leap in productivity of 15 per cent.

That such benefits are much more likely to outlast the downturn, after which companies can really harvest the opportunities provided by the recession, is highlighted by Ford, which took advantage of the auto industry downturn a decade ago to improve vastly its decision structure. By the mid-1980s, despite its rival General Motors (GM) having spent more than three times as much as Ford on plant and equipment, Ford had caught up with GM in both market value and profits, and had taken market share from GM.

Improved negotiations with unions

'Times have changed', declared Douglas Fraser, president of the United Auto Workers union in the US, when a decade ago his union dropped its opposition to contract negotiations in the auto industry.

Companies tend to find unions less of a restricting influence when trying to increase productivity in difficult times. Downturns are clearly the time to push through measures to improve efficiency. There are several reasons why unions are quiescent in this period.

Union membership has continued to drop substantially in much of the West. In just five years in the 1980s, union membership in the US fell by over a sixth. Indeed, the rapid rise of service industries which are predominantly non-unionized (because of short-term career attitudes, alleged chauvinism of unions to female workers, and the expense of reaching members in temporary jobs) has led to unions having to amalgamate to grow, increase their power and spread their overheads across more members. Such distractions offer opportunities.

Wage and benefit 'give-backs' begin to appear in a downturn as management exploits these pressures to improve the company. General Electric (GE) in the US is well known for this approach. In fact, GE union membership has almost halved since the 1960s. The head of the International Union of Electrical Workers at GE, William Bywater, explained: 'Our philosophy is that it makes no sense to win huge wage increases if our members aren't going to have a job in six months.'

Similarly, at its Saturn project, General Motors was able to negotiate 20 per cent lower compensation packages for its workforce by offering them permanent job security and the right to be involved in major decisions.

Introducing pay-for-performance policies has been aided by the distraction: a survey of 600 companies in the US showed that some 20 per cent had exploited the gap to push through such pay policies, with another 33 per cent intending to do so.

Companies have sometimes been forced to renege on contracts. Some argue that national contracts which pay uniform wages are inappropriate because of differences in product lines. The decentralization of business units, it has also been argued, called for wages specific to a region and industry. Cost of living allowances, negotiated in better times, are often among the first contractual conditions to go. The entire white collar staff of General Motors was once told that the company could no longer afford automatic cost-of-living allowances.

A salutary case of the increasing difficulty of such approaches is that of the UK aero-engine manufacturer Rolls-Royce. Over one weekend in 1991 the company sent out dismissal notices to all its 34,000 workers. It then offered all the workers their old jobs back, but subject to altered contracts which specified a six-month freeze on pay, and rewards for service, age and skills. This move, a company spokesman exclaimed, was 'purely a technicality to ensure that we are not in breach of contract'. Union leaders were outraged by the lack of consultation in combination with the 51 per cent rise in the chairman's salary (later changed to a 10 per cent cut) and the already announced 6000 redundancies. In the face of threatened legal action, Rolls-Royce withdrew the dismissal notices and began negotiations with the employees.

Achieving good deals from unions can also be due to a change of attitude among them. Moving from the adversarial approach to the partnership ideal is the UK's Electrical, Electronic, Plumbing and Telecommunications Union (EEPTU). Its chief, Eric Hammond, declared that: 'I believe we must work positively for proper rewards for our members, but this means boosting profits'. The EEPTU has been instrumental in introducing to the UK the innovations of non-strike agreements, pendulum arbitration and single-union deals.

The advent of non-strike agreements, particularly in Japanese manufacturing companies in the UK, has given rise among the union's rank and file of the accusation of a sell-out of its ultimate sanction of withdrawing its labour. However, the union leadership is adamant that non-strike agreements are in the best interest of its members. EEPTU's rival AEU (Association of Electrical Engineers) has extended the no-strike agreements to non-Japanese companies with a three-year agreement at Coca-Cola & Schweppes Beverages's new Wakefield plant.

Another innovation is the acceptance by both parties of the pendulum arbitration method where an independent arbitrator must come out in favour of one side or another. In this way, both management and union demands must be realistic in order to be acceptable. Outrageous demands by either side, in order to pull a compromise solution more towards each parties' desired solution have been made a thing of the past.

Single-union agreements, giving sole bargaining rights to one union, have helped Toshiba to make speedy decisions and to increase its flexibility. A trade union official is in favour of the move to one union: '[in the past] there were so many unions, you could argue as much between unions as with management.'

The advisability of so-called 'union bashing' is something which should be carefully thought about, as seen at Ford's Jaguar Cars where a union leader, after a cut in the workforce some years ago, was overheard to say, 'It's your turn now, just wait until it's ours'.

The aim of taking advantage of the pressure of unions should not be to squeeze the pips until they squeak. The benefits in a cooperative relationship with the workforce must not be lost. 'If they drive too hard a bargain on wages', wrote Albert Rees, author of *Economics of Trade Unions*, 'there may be effects on productivity which mean they haven't gained much.'

Breaking strikes

There will be times when the need of the organization to improve productivity and to downsize is such that negotiations break down and employees apply the ultimate sanction of withdrawing their labour.

Strikes are expensive for both the company and the workers, and arguments for persuading the unions not to strike can be convincing. Because unemployment increases in a recession, employers can use the threat of unemployment to push through unpopular policies. Traditionally, workers have been reluctant to strike when the main issue has been that of security; in fact, it has been shown that strikes over wages are over ten times as likely as strikes over security.

While strikes build a great deal of animosity which may have lingering adverse effects on the company, the cost of giving concessions may well outbalance the cost of the strike. However, with public approval of unions down, union membership low, and new legal measures against secondary strike tactics, the cost of breaking strikes can be cheaper than giving into them.

After everything reasonable has been done to avert the strike, the company should consider pushing through with the opportunity to reduce costs and, if a strike should occur, to break the strike. Strikes can be prepared for – using a combative approach. Tenneco and Phelps Dodge are good examples.

Tenneco. Edward Campbell, head of Tenneco's Newport News Shipbuilding company, learned in late 1978 that his 16,000 workers would be on strike within a month. He quickly developed a strike contingency plan so that, when the workers went out on strike, Campbell was able to keep the plant going by deploying supervisory employees and office workers. By the second week, 20 per cent of the strikers were back; by the ninth week, 70 per cent had returned. It was all over after 12 weeks. Campbell's strategy had paid off.

Phelps Dodge, the large copper combine, broke a strike to cut its costs. When its contract with United Steel Workers (USW) expired in mid-1983, the chairman, George Monroe, told them that the company could no longer afford the contractual cost-of-living adjustments which had driven wages up 30 per cent over two years, while copper prices had fallen 28 per cent. The USW went on strike, but Phelps was able to break it. Phelps Dodge is now reported to have one of the lowest labour costs and lowest overall costs in the US copper industry.

Downsizing

Laying people off is something that managers naturally want to avoid. The sheer expense of hiring people in a boom, the difficulty of hiring them (because of adverse demographics, skill shortages and increased competition for good staff in an upswing), and the waste of training and knowledge investment, all these should make managers think twice about firing people. An unusual public commitment to its employees was once made by Ford, where the UK director of operations was quoted as saying that the company would rather earn lower profits than make staff redundant because it felt that laying workers off would damage the credibility of its efforts to encourage loyalty and commitment to quality.

In fact, cutting labour costs by lay-offs or wage freezes may not be the most appropriate response to a downturn for some companies. The proportion of costs due to people is sometimes surprisingly small, a fact often even more surprisingly overlooked by management. While this percentage is approximately 65 per cent for advertising companies, for manufacturing companies it can be as low as 15 per cent.

Only when all the above approaches have been considered, and found not to be sufficient, is it time to consider reductions in employee numbers.

Adversity often provides the opportunity and the spur as ICI's example shows.

> **ICI.** A study of the number of employees at ICI 'reveals that ICI have tended to be most effective in reducing their numbers of UK employees in the years when they could argue their business performance was not good'. Those years have clearly been 1970–72 and 1979–83, when staff reductions of 7 and 33 per cent respectively were effected.

When cutting jobs and plants it is important to ensure that your actions correspond with what has been communicated or implied to third parties. Failure to observe extreme care in such communications can leave you open to charges of unethical behaviour. A salutary lesson is provided by the experience of General Motors. GM, an important employer in the town of Norwood, Ohio, decided to close a factory and to pull out of the area. At the time of closure the local authority was reported to have considered claiming substantial damages against GM for what it saw as abandoning commitments made to the community regarding the plant staying open.

Act decisively

'The only way to swallow a bitter mixture is to swallow it in a single gulp,' wrote Churchill. Dribbling out the lay-offs is not inspiring to employees. Senior managers are seen as the culprits for getting the company into the mess and are blamed for hesitating over necessary action.

While it is an unpleasant personal task to release people, it should be seen as being in the best interests of the company: the greatest good for the greatest number. In the words of a partner in a large insolvency practice: 'It is a purely clinical exercise done to try to save the company. If it is not done, it is possible everybody's job will be lost.'

Part of acting decisively is acting faster than the competition to take advantage of the benefits before the competition. At Rolls-Royce, the UK aero-engine manufacturer, the chief executive, Sir Ralph Robins, remarked on announcing redundancies and extensive cost-cutting measures: 'I worry we reacted perhaps too slowly.' Its competitors, General Electric and Pratt and Whitney in the US, had responded to the worldwide slow-down in orders by initiating their restructuring rather earlier.

Many staff are likely to feel demotivated at the prospect of reduced salaries and the diminished opportunity for promotion in a contracting company. Older staff tend to reciprocate previous good company relations through the bad times and stay. But younger managers have less of an emotional commitment to the company and may consider leaving. Hence, it is vital to ensure that, where their prospects are being blocked by the presence of incompetents, it is the dead wood which goes, and which is seen to go.

Showing you care (and meaning it)

This attitude demonstrates a moral obligation to those departing and makes clear to the survivors that they are valued team members. 'IBMers', for example, are almost invariably proud of, and loyal to, their company. One of the reasons for this is that IBM tries hard to take care of its people. 'We always try to deploy redundant employees elsewhere in the enterprise', reported an IBM Europe president.

When IBM was forced to make 14,000 people redundant, it initiated a pilot scheme of offering a fixed amount of freelance consultancy work to its longer-serving senior staff. In this way the company was able to make use of the employees' skills while providing a useful fee-paying transition for the employees.

Dana Corporation, a leading US auto parts manufacturer, has often been held up as holding a similarly enlightened attitude. Having held high for many years its 'philosophy of continued employment for all Dana people', the company was forced to change tack in the early 1980s when a disastrous foray into a new market led to the closure of several plants and the need to lay off a third of its near 30,000 workforce. Dana offered preferential hiring at other plants, handed lists of the out-of-work around other local manufacturers, and began a job-counselling programme. Dana, believed an ex-employee, 'went the extra mile'.

Cutting indirect labour costs

The main opportunity to cut labour costs tends to occur in the indirect areas. Traditionally, overhead costs have received little attention compared to direct costs. However, as technology changes, and service becomes an ever more important competitive edge, so indirect costs will tend to expand to a greater percentage of total costs.

Some companies have become aware of the potential for cost-cutting in indirect areas. Detroit Trim and People Express illustrate this well.

Detroit Trim, the Chrysler subsidiary in the early 1980s, was forced to make some of its employees redundant in its fight for survival. An analysis of the lay-offs showed that 25 per cent of its salaried employees and 21 per cent of its production workers were made redundant. Yet it was found that there was so much inefficiency in the indirect departments that a full 40 per cent of its indirect employees could be removed.

US airlines. The US airline industry, after deregulation, demonstrated many different approaches to reducing indirect and fixed labour costs. People Express (PE) emerged as a major player with much lower costs, particularly labour costs. PE was able to offer a low base salary because it wasn't unionized, and because it offered extensive profit-sharing and stock options. In addition, due to the conditions in the industry at the time, there was a pool of unemployed yet highly skilled airline staff who welcomed the opportunity to join a fast growing company with an exciting high profile for low or deferred rewards. The following figures are an indication of the power of the PE approach: pilots for Eastern Airlines were reported at one time to have made $140,000 for 564 hours flying, while pilots for PE earned $55,000 for 900 hours.

Disappearance of middle managers

The appearance over the last decade of new technologies has made many jobs and even departments redundant. In addition, owing to the drop in the cost of computers, many more applications have opened up. Now that many more computer-literate executives are in office, improved communications allow top decision-makers to maintain control without the need for filtering by middle management. Taken together, these facts spell the emergence of companies making large-scale lay-offs of white collar staff. An example of such an organization is BP.

BP. At its Standard Oil subsidiary in the US, BP chairman, Robert Horton, reduced 11 layers of management to just five. Employing the same strategy at BP in the UK, he sees it not so much as a cost-cutting exercise as an effort to improve the management of the company by reducing its complexity and changing its corporate style.

The aim is to simplify and accelerate decision-making while devolving more responsibility and authority to individual managers. Horton described the laid-off managers as the 'brigadier belt', 'whose sole purpose in life is to act as blotting paper. They prevent information coming down from the top.' By writing off and selling unproductive assets, Horton had turned Standard's loss of $242 million to a $564 million profit in 18 months.

There are further benefits extending beyond costs and flexibility. An ex-manager at BP believes 'BP management has done exactly the right thing. You need a turnover of people to create the values and culture of the new [revitalized] company.'

Two-tier wage structure

While flying in the face of 'equal pay for equal work' in the mid-1980s, almost 10 per cent of corporations in the US possessed major union contracts which contained clauses allowing newly hired people to be paid less than the existing workers. One of the best-known exponents of such a two-tier wage structure is the US airline Pan-Am.

Pan-Am. C Edward Acker, the chief executive officer of Pan-Am in those days, was forced to respond to the competition by People Express. He responded by initially cutting the workforce by 10 per cent through the expedient of halving the legal and public relations departments, and chopping out layers of supervisory management. But by 1981 Pan-Am was near bankruptcy and was losing $1 million per day. The unions accepted 10 per cent wage cuts, aware that the company might go under. Next year, they conceded a wage freeze in return for 10 per cent of the company's stock. Non-flying assets like the Pan-Am building in New York had to be sold.

But Pan-Am's labour costs were still too high. So a two-tier wage rate was introduced, with newly hired people, to replace natural wastage, receiving a lower wage than the existing workforce. In this way, it was hoped that it would not be necessary to abrogate or renegotiate contracts to reduce wages for the people already there.

Core and temporaries

Some companies have reorganized their structure around what they're really good at ('the core'), supported by contracted or temporary 'support' staff. The core consists of the 'knowledge' workers who have acquired specific skills which cannot be easily replaced. The support workers have much less specific skills. In such a structured company, if cuts in personnel have to be made, the company tries to protect its life-blood of core workers first; in a downturn, cost savings come from releasing the support staff, where possible.

The Japanese are renowned (or notorious) for their adoption of this technique. They seem to be remarkably adept at using temporary staff. They subcontract work on the explicit understanding that a permanent relationship is not implied. They offer work to retirees on short-term assignments at lower salaries, and housewives are hired in overload conditions, on the clear understanding that the company will keep them on only while it needs them.

Reducing working hours and pay are approaches used in Japan as in the West. In addition, pay is controlled by offering semi-annual bonuses whose value is linked to profits – these may go down as well as up. Some firms have even asked employees to take immediate vacations with partial rather than full pay. A novel idea that I've never heard used here is to proffer minor salary cuts to workers while higher-level managers are forced to accept larger salary cuts.

More hours, same pay; less hours, less pay

We have already explored the idea of getting more work out of people for the same number of hours. Another option is getting more hours for the same pay. The crisis mentality imbued in the workforce, combined with loyalty to the company and team workers, makes this possible, as exemplified by the successful turnaround of Wickes in the US. When Wickes, the large US retailer, filed for Chapter 11 protection from its creditors, the new chief executive officer, Sigoloff, warned his co-workers, 'If you work here, it's six days work for five days' pay'.

Another way to cut labour costs is to cut the working week to, say, three days temporarily, with a concomitant cut in salary. People loyal to the company who can be persuaded that it is in their best interests to stay will live with the situation.

Chapter 11 as management strategy

'Chapter 11', a judge was heard to say, 'is becoming an effective management strategy.' Chapter 11, the application to a court by a US company for protection from its creditors while it restructures (and need not pay interest charges), is certainly becoming more common. Its UK equivalent is 'Administration', which was introduced in the Insolvency Act of 1986.

Originally designed for companies in imminent danger of sliding into bankruptcy, its uses are becoming much wider, as the examples of Wilson and Continental Air demonstrate.

Wilson, the largest pork-processing company in the US, had just been spun off from LTV in 1981 when it filed for Chapter 11, declaring union contracts to be 80 per cent costlier than those of its competition. Just hours after filing, Wilson had abrogated contracts and slashed wages in half. The union went out on strike, but not long after signed the management contracts. Wilson had therefore much reduced its labour costs considerably by entering Chapter 11.

Continental Air. Perhaps the most notorious exponent of the Chapter 11 strategy is Frank Lorenzo. When his competitor, Braniff, filed for Chapter 11 with over 4000 lay-offs, Lorenzo warned his people 'what happened to Braniff is going to continue to discipline the industry'. A year later, Lorenzo's Continental entered Chapter 11, declaring labour costs to be twice the national average. The company laid off 65 per cent of its employees and cut pay in half. Just two years later, Continental had doubled its traffic and declared the biggest profits in its 50-year history. The Chapter 11 move was a linchpin in its successful recovery strategy.

Chapter 6

Improving Cash Flow

Saving cash for other battles

Difficult conditions provide the opportunity to steal a march over the competition in many ways. Better cash-flow management is one of them. A company that gets its cash flow right is not only saving the cash for other battles, but is also providing itself with the opportunity to do better than the competition. This chapter gives a brief outline of how to make the most of the opportunities to improve cash flow.

Cash flow differs from profits in that there is a time-lag between the laying out of the cost of goods and receiving the revenue. This period is extended in a downturn. Since everyone is short of cash, customers try to hang on to what they have as long as possible to ease their cash scheduling. As a result, customers pass on their cash-flow problems to you. Those customers with a lot of buying power over you (that is, large companies, those who represent a major proportion of supplies or sales, or those who have some other strategically important relationship) are particularly prone to this. Small companies therefore find themselves being squeezed by the big companies.

Putting out the fire

The standard advice is that immediate cash-flow improvements derive from cut-price sale of inventory, changing employment contracts, renegotiating interest payments, encouraging customers to pay more quickly, persuading suppliers to accept delayed payment and, of course, reducing purchases. Allowing a small (a few per cent, say) discount for invoices paid before their due dates can be beneficial too.

Factoring

A well-known but still underused method for improving cash flow is factoring a company's accounts receivable. Since such debtors represent about 40 per cent of the value of most trading companies, and their collection can generate many operational difficulties, factoring has proved immensely useful to many companies. By selling the invoices to a third party, who then collects the money and is responsible for bad debts, you can receive 80 per cent of the face value of the invoice within a few days. Getting the money at least 30 days, and commonly 45 days, earlier than you would have done, with the balance (less a fee) paid on maturity, is a very important method of increasing cash flow. Such administration of the sales ledger, protection against bad debt, finance against sales invoices can be expensive, however.

Areas not usually considered suitable for factoring include high-technology products, products sold on consignment with a right of return, some service companies, partial payment contractors (in the building sector, for instance) and where profit margins are low.

Factoring is particularly suitable for financing explosive growth, protecting against bad debts in a recession, and coping with sudden changes in inflation.

Leaseback

Many companies which have a significant proportion of their capital tied up in assets have used the leaseback method to great success in releasing much needed funds. Selling the assets and then leasing them back allows the company to continue to use them while also providing a large one-off injection of funds (maybe $100 million for a large building, for example). Buildings, plant and even equipment which the company may be leasing out to customers, all can be used in a leaseback arrangement.

An additional advantage is the release of valuable management time which would provide better shareholder value by concentrating on the core activities of the company.

Keeping tabs on the inventory

Reducing inventory and work in progress provides one of the fastest opportunities for providing cash for restructuring. A recent survey showed that levels of inventory in the UK manufacturing industry are up to twice those of the best global competition.

Keeping an eye on inventory also builds awareness of the carrying costs of that inventory, which are mainly dependent on the cost of having money tied up in periods of high interest rates. High interest rates make low levels of inventory and work-in-progress mandatory.

Inflation tends to increase the working capital requirements of inventory and accounts receivable (debtors). Moving to a LIFO (last-in, first out) costing system can help a company to keep up to date on the true value of its inventory. In the LIFO system, as opposed to the alternative FIFO (first-in, first-out) system, each sale of a product from inventory reduces the stock value by the current (inflated) cost of making the product, rather than historical costs. In this way the value of the inventory more accurately reflects the effect of inflation. However, an unfortunate side-effect of accounting conventions is that moving from a FIFO to a LIFO costing system wipes out the so-called inventory profit, where selling older product valued at historical costs appears to generate higher margins.

Improving control over inventory brings down the stock:sales ratio, reducing the need for sudden cuts in production when demand slows.

An example of a company which successfully reduced inventory and work-in-progress is Wadkin.

> **Wadkin,** the leading wood-working machinery manufacturer in the UK, was able to free some £2 million by cutting work in progress by £1.3 million in one year, while reducing inventory of raw materials, finished and bought-in goods released another £0.6 million. This was then invested in machinery which allowed it to build profits substantially and hold on to its market share.

Just-in-time

The aims of just-in-time (JIT) are to try to match perfectly the output to the market demands. Waste, which adds costs but not value (reworking, inspection, waiting and work-in-progress, for instance), should be eliminated. The thesis is that high levels of inventory hide fundamental problems which, by using smaller safety margins, could be identified by the bottle-necks that appear.

One way of reducing the carrying costs of inventory is to carry less of it. The most common concept of JIT is putting pressure on suppliers. Persuading suppliers to deliver just-in-time, or JIT, puts the carrying costs and hidden administration costs on them.

There is also scope for improvements in cash flow from internal JIT. Companies sometimes deliberately carry high levels of inventory as an 'insurance premium' against stock-outs, which would damage their record of deliveries. An example of JIT in action is that of Knowle Electronics.

> **Knowle Electronics,** a UK manufacturer of small microphones and receivers for hearing aids, was pressed for even shorter deliveries. Having

> prided itself on its delivery performance, the company embarked on an investigation of how it could improve. To some surprise, the managing director found that it carried 12 weeks' worth of stock, work-in-progress (WIP), materials and bought-in parts. The result was that, within three months, Knowle Electronics had managed to work its WIP down to just a third of its former levels.

Paying later

It is well known that larger companies respond to pressures from their customers by paying their bills much later to small companies. Figures collected by Intrum Justitia [3], Europe's largest debt-reduction company, indicated that even though standard business terms in the UK are 30 days, a typical small business waits a further 48 days for receipt of payment.

Paying your bills a little later is therefore a recognized tactic. The extra cost imposed by the supplier for late payment has to be balanced against the extra benefit of having the cash for a little longer. It is rare that a supplier will claim interest charges, unless he has negotiated it beforehand, although in parts of continental Europe the right to claim interest charges on overdue bills is enshrined in law.

A supplier may even be pressured into offering later payment to win an order, in which case it acts as a price cut substitute.

The customer pays first

This is the classic business strategy – getting the customer to do all the financing. Consider retail food chains which sell most of their food within a few days of receiving it. Most of these payments are in cash, or are paid within a few days. Yet the food chains do not have to pay their suppliers for 30 days or more, during which time they have the use of the money.

Another example is provided by my local gas supply company. It offers me the choice of paying for my gas in equal amounts over the year by direct debit from my bank account. The launch of this scheme was held in the early summer, yet the major gas usage would be in the winter. Hence, not only does the gas company have a steady stream of revenue with smaller collection costs, but it also has a positive cash flow, with revenue being received before the expenditure on its supply.

Can the customer be persuaded to pay up front? Will he take cash on delivery, rather than the usual invoice and extended credit period? Might he agree to pay by standing order?

Controlling debtor risk

Recessions lead to an increased risk of defaulting. All companies are more vulnerable to nasty surprises in a recession. Possible catastrophes can be avoided by being aware of the latest status of each debtor. Reviewing information frequently and concentrating on the most important debtors are key factors.

Trade insurance can provide up to 80 per cent of the invoice value in the event of insolvency of the customer. Since receivables account for 40 per cent of the net worth of a typical trading company, trade insurance can be a useful hedge.

Leasing

Leasing can increase flexibility and certainly aids cash flow in reducing the up-front investment, as illustrated by the example of commercial aircraft where the volatility of demand, the vulnerability of fuel costs to oil shocks, and the high fixed cost of aircraft have persuaded many airlines to lease their aircraft. Indeed, some 17 per cent of the world's fleet is leased, which allows airlines to reduce their capacity quickly if necessary.

Part III
Competitive Marketing

Chapters 7 and 8 deal with techniques for increasing demand by selling to existing customers and new customers respectively. These are followed by two chapters dealing with the critical element of price. Chapter 9 concerns the key lessons of avoiding the slide into price cuts by raising the perception of the value of the product in the customers' eyes. Chapter 10 details techniques for disguising price cuts and using low price as a competitive weapon.

Opportunities

Discard hard and fast rules. Victory is the only thing that matters, and this cannot be achieved by adhering to conventional canons.

Sun Tzu

Downturns provide the greatest opportunity

Since the old ways aren't working, customers are awake to new ideas. For companies which are able to look at their products and what their customers want in a different way, a downturn offers many opportunities. As old relationships unfreeze and new relationships are built, companies can lock out their competitors in the lucrative upturn.

By making the most of their existing customers, companies can ensure a continuing source of revenue and prevent their loss to competitors. By offering customers existing products in a new or better way, new products or a new form of partnership, companies can rewrite the rules and exploit the opportunity provided by the downturn.

New products can steal a march on the competition. New ways of selling products into new markets can capture market share and profits.

Companies can wrong-foot competitors and build margins by avoiding price cuts and price wars, or use their lower cost bases to win a greater market share and eliminate the competition.

Chapter 7

Making the Most of Existing Customers

Like filling a bath with the plug out

Every company is concerned with increasing sales and market share. Yet most companies think only of winning new customers, so they inadvertently adopt the short-sighted policy of not looking after their existing customers, and therefore lose them at a significant rate. Seeking new customers in this case has been described as 'trying to fill a bath with the plug out'.

It is truly surprising how many companies, in their search for sales, overlook the importance of their existing customers – a vast reservoir of additional revenue available at little cost. When you consider the low conversion rates of each marketing effort into leads to quotes to orders, and the marketing costs and the time-lag associated with winning a new customer, the gestation period of the decision and then the delay in getting paid, it makes sense to focus on existing customers.

This chapter demonstrates the three key strategies for exploiting the opportunities presented by existing customers: focusing on customers with the greatest potential, building up a stable stream of revenue, and managing the value of an end-product in partnership with suppliers and customers.

Go where the money is

The essence of the strategy to win sales from existing customers has been encapsulated by a certain bank robber who, when asked how he chose his targets, said, 'I go where the money is, and I go there often.'

A manager should be aware of the importance of focusing the organization's efforts on where they have a powerful impact – or else he should expect to be fired. From the scale of company failures and mass redundancies of managers in a downturn, it is clear that many managers just do not focus.

Setting priorities is one of the main functions of a manager, yet many people spend their professional and personal lives on 'busy work' of low priority which is easy to do. Such activity gives the person a feeling of accomplishment, but the important work which would add to the profits of the company remains undone. The same process applies to targeting marketing efforts.

This section explains some of the considerations involved in winning sales from existing customers in straitened times. Many of these ideas will be directly applicable to the quest for new customers as well.

Customers with the greatest ability to buy

Targeting the company's marketing at those customers who are best placed to buy and doing it cost effectively is key. To do this, it is necessary to identify customers for whom profits or disposable income remain high and steady, largely unaffected by a downturn, and then target your efforts at them. For example, consider a chief executive who wishes to reach the 1 million customers who are able to buy his product. He could try a mass advertising campaign covering 100 million people and costing, say, 10 cents per person (total cost $10 million), but his campaign might be more successful and more cost-effective if he used direct mailing to the 1 million potential customers at, say, $3 per person (total cost $3 million). Alternatively, he might look at special interest magazines, cable TV or the regional press, for example.

Customers for whom your product is best suited

A company's marketing will be most effective if customers are offered only what they are going to want. Customers should therefore be grouped and prioritized by their needs. Products can then be better positioned to maximize their appeal to each customer segment. One of the best examples of such an approach is Fingerhut.

Fingerhut is a well-known US supplier of household and consumer goods by mail order. By targeting its products and mailings, it managed to improve its profits in the very depths of recession.

Analyzing its database of customers, made up of questionnaire replies and records of purchases, the marketing department was able to develop a profile of each of its customers. By studying the effects of the previous recession on sales to the customer base, Fingerhut could track the incoming recession and predict the behaviour of groups of customers. This information then became the basis of a concerted marketing strategy.

Sales to marginal customers whose records suggested that they might have trouble making payments were curtailed. The product mix was reoriented from 'big ticket' items to less expensive products. While the number of mailings to areas of higher unemployment was reduced, mailings to the better-off customers were increased and credit extended. These customers were further targeted with a telephone campaign in order to generate a higher response and pitch for more sales.

By recognizing the need to focus on where the money is, Fingerhut was able to reap the reward of increased profits.

Customers with the greatest insensitivity to price

As it makes sense to target customers who are insensitive to price, companies should be looking for applications where the cost of their product is a small percentage of the customer's total costs.

Companies need to identify customers for whom the perceived *value* of the product far outweighs the *price*. These companies will also be insensitive to price. Such customers include those for whom the product will make a great deal more money than they need to lay out, or provide a competitive edge over their competitors, or satisfy an important desire which cannot be easily satisfied any other way, or prevent a catastrophic loss.

A supplier of printing machines which mark every food product coming off a production line with the legally required 'sell by' date uses this approach to maintain large margins. Failure of the machine would cost the food manufacturer a fortune in down-time. Hence, the customer rates reliability as the number one priority on his ranking of purchase criteria. He does not baulk at paying a premium for a machine with features to enhance reliability, or a large charge for regular servicing. He may even be happy to buy a spare machine and to keep it running on stand-by, just in case of breakdown.

Customers who are unaware of alternatives are often insensitive to price and can provide an opportunity. Companies should therefore identify customers who lack information, or the inclination to gather information, on substitutes or competing products.

In China, where business practices appear to be rather sharper than in the West, there is an old proverb which says, 'If there is a hole in the carpet do not point it out, but put your foot over it'.

Customers who are locked into your products

Identify those customers for whom the cost of switching to an alternative would be too high and then concentrate marketing efforts on them.

Enumerate the significant switching costs the customer would face if he went elsewhere and make him aware of them (subtly!). These might include the costs of replacing incompatible software, retraining, write-off of investment, dual inventory of spare parts, and the costs of management being distracted from the operation of the company.

You need to emphasize the time and effort required for a customer to evaluate fully the alternatives, and point out the downside risks of going for a solution of unknown quality. Many companies, eager for new business, are less than scrupulous in their promises. The supplier recognizes that once the customer has changed to him, he will be emotionally locked in, despite the supplier's inability to meet promises of delivery, service and quality.

A policy of designing your products so that they possess inherent high switching costs can bear fruit. Making your products incompatible with those of competitors, or building in a proprietary element which cannot be easily reproduced, are possible strategies. Naturally, customers do not like being locked in, therefore companies need to provide sufficient benefits to overcome this aversion.

IBM's mainframe computer strategy has been considered the archetype of this concept for some years. By using proprietary 'closed' hardware and software, IBM has ensured an exclusive market. If customers require additional pieces of hardware for their IBM mainframe systems (for upgrades, for example), they have had to obtain them from IBM. More importantly, having customized their software for an IBM computer, and organized their information in a certain way, customers would clearly be enormously disadvantaged if they wanted to change to a non-compatible computer system.

In another case, the chief executive of a company which provided highly skilled servicing and the supply of consumables for a complex computerized machine discovered that he had been 'holding up a price umbrella' on his consumables. His prices were so high that customers were refilling their machines themselves. In addition, a competitor was helping customers to do this, and in the process was taking over 20 per cent of the supplier's profits. The solution employed by the supplier was to declare that no service would be provided for machines which had not used the supplier's consumables, moving to sealed cartridges, building in security circuits into the containers, and differentiating the company's consumables from competing products by explaining their relative advantages.

Switching costs have long been a successful basis for the highly profitable combination of both repeat and recurring revenue.

The three Rs

Generating stable and continuing revenue is a clear imperative for companies in a downturn. The three generic strategies are generating repeat business and recurring revenue, and maximizing the number of bites of the cherry by using referrals aggressively. These three Rs will now be examined in turn.

Repeat business

Repeat business – persuading existing customers to buy more product from you – must be carefully nurtured in a downturn. Such a strategy depends on demonstrating the advantages of the customer staying with your company, exciting him with the idea of buying more product, and persuading him to look at upgrading or trading-up. Of these, the most important factor in generating repeat business is taking care of your customer.

Take care of your customers

If customers are kept happy, they'll keep coming back for more. Although this may seem an obvious paradigm, it is often tragically overlooked. Companies need to show their face to solicit feedback, and to resell the customer on the company and the relative advantages of the company's products.

Theodore Levitt of the Harvard Business School likens the customer–supplier relationship to that of marriage. Courtship leads to the first sale but it is the quality of the marriage that follows which determines whether 'there will be contentment and expanded business or trouble and divorce'. Lack of communication tolls the death knell for many marriages; that this is also true for business partnerships is highlighted by the opportunity discovered by Nationwide Anglia. What does it say about your competitors, for instance, when you find that fully 40 per cent of your customers have come from rivals – and this in an industry where lifetime loyalty is the norm? Yet this was the very experience of Nationwide Anglia, a prominent retail financial institution in Britain. Obviously, its competitors were unaware of their customers' needs, or were unable to take care of them.

Ask, do, tell

Companies often become caught in a vicious circle where sales and service personnel tend to be reluctant to solicit feedback because they fear receiving a rap on the knuckles, involving them in additional and often unappreciated work, as the benefits of customer care are difficult to quantify against costs. Only the courage of a determined and uncompromising chief executive can lead a company out of such a damaging and ultimately fatal attitude.

The only possible answer is to raise the priority of customer care, ensuring that customers are happy with the service they receive. The leader must encourage his people to show their face as often as possible, soliciting feedback frequently and in depth. Customers must be made to feel that it is worthwhile to be open and honest: they often feel the effort to be of little benefit to them and are reluctant to hurt the feelings of the suppliers' personnel. They have to see the results of their efforts and that you really care.

'Ask, do, tell' are the watchwords. Ask them what you could do better, then do it. Then tell them what you have done. IBM is a company which recognizes the importance of meeting its customers' needs better. Its former president, Jack Kuehler, was concerned about the need for his employees to stay close to the marketplace. 'Get out of your offices', he said to them. 'Find out what you're doing right. Find out what you're doing wrong. Do something about it.'

Some companies become complacent when they have been serving their customers for many years, and when they do not feel under competitive pressure. They feel that their service cannot be improved. To these people I quote Henry Horrower: 'It is always safer to assume, not that the old way is wrong, but that there might be a better way.' Don't assume therefore that because they don't tell you, there isn't a problem.

Consider the case of Sir John Quinton, the chairman of Barclays Bank, one of the 'Big Four' banks in the UK. Disturbed by a press campaign against banks' alleged arrogance towards their small business customers, he exclaimed that since only 1 per cent of his bank's small business customers had written to him, he could assume that the other 99 per cent were reasonably happy with the bank. Yet a MORI survey published that week showed that over 20 per cent of small business customers were dissatisfied with their banks while over 50 per cent said their banks didn't understand them. It is small wonder then that on-the-ball competitors can profit from such an opportunity to attract disgruntled customers.

There will be times when it won't be enough to talk to several customers; instead, it may be necessary to collect information on a more systematic basis, as illustrated by Burger King's experience.

Burger King. When Barry Gibbons took over at Burger King, he felt that there was a vast multitude of problems which needed to be cleared up. However, he needed to know which were the most important for his customers and which had to be solved first. So he set up employee and supplier surveys, and a freefone number for customers to call in with their comments. He also hired people from outside the company to visit the restaurants on a regular basis as 'mystery shoppers' to give him their independent impressions. In this way, he was able to receive 80,000 'snapshots' of the company every month.

From this information, he was able to work out which of the company's problems needed most attention. This led to the elimination of substandard stores and the refurbishment of restaurants. Quality was improved and new product development was instigated to fill perceived gaps shown up by competitors. One of the new lines was to prove highly significant for Burger King. Skipping the traditional 18 months of customer tests, and ignoring roars of protest from his marketing department, Barry Gibbons launched the 'BK Broiler' ('BK Flamer' in the UK) chicken sandwich in 1990. Within three months it was achieving sustained sales of over one million units a day. Annual profits rose by 23 per cent and Barry Gibbons made the cover of *Fortune* magazine.

Give them what they want

It really is quite remarkable how short-sighted some firms can be. Indeed, some companies are capable of substantially increasing their sales to customers yet are totally unaware of it. Consider the company which, while actively searching for new business opportunities, had overlooked that it was actually losing close to 15 per cent of its sales through short deliveries to its customers. In the boom time of several years before, the salespeople had been instructed to ration the supply of product. But with the arrival of straitened times, the company was looking to fill its capacity, yet its customers had got used to ordering only a limited amount from that company, using other sources for the rest. In this case, it was a consultant who was able to approach the situation from a different viewpoint and see the folly of the company's marketing efforts.

Some companies are unable to define their customer segments. But to satisfy customers' needs, customer groups must be identified and their needs established. SAS is a classic example of a company which finds out what its customers want and then gives it to them.

SAS, the Scandinavian airline company, was successfully turned around by Jan Carlzon, whose first action was to conduct an extensive poll among business customers, the favoured target segment. Their main concern, they said, was 'knowing the planes would leave on time'. Carlzon, who had defined SAS's mission as 'the best airline for the frequent business traveller', more specifically ensured that SAS built a reputation as the airline which leaves on time.

He communicated this message to his staff in the legendary little red books given to each employee: 'Let's get in there and fight' and 'The fight of the century'. He showed that employees, when they are clear about the goals of the company and know that they will get the support of top management, will show ingenuity and commitment beyond their best expectations.

It was to discovering and communicating the mission in simple and unambiguous terms that SAS owes its spectacular recovery.

Taking care of your customers and giving them what they want means segmenting them into groups: those who require extensive support, those who are more keen on a lower price (and for whom support should be reduced to maintain margins), and those who it will not be economical to sell to.

Upgrading

Upgrading, or trading up, is a form of repeat purchase. It is clearly in a company's interest not only to encourage a customer to come back and buy again, but also to persuade him to replace his product with a higher-specification product, as the following example illustrates.

Gulfstream. Allen Paulson, as a private investor, had just acquired Gulfstream Aerospace, the ailing US manufacturer of business jets, and was keen to repay debt and to turn around the company's performance. He found that, by offering the Gulfstream III model to Gulfstream II owners, he was able to capture a windfall of $18 million in new revenues. This was a significant amount for a company losing $2 million a day at the time.

Built-in obsolescence, or the rapid improvement of a product's features by the use of a new form of technology, can provide similar revenue. New generations of computers, for example, are so powerful compared to previous models that customers can justify the expense of new models by the resulting efficiency gains. One of the arch exponents of this strategy in the past has been General Motors (GM).

General Motors. Since the 1930s, GM's strategy has been to offer a range of models to suit every pocket. In this way, it was hoped that the customer would stay with GM all his life, thereby maximizing repeat business.

The rationale behind this strategy is as follows. As the customer earned more, his aspirations would change, and so he would want to upgrade his automobile. He would then trade up from a GM Chevrolet to a GM Buick to a GM Oldsmobile to a GM Cadillac. The former chairman, Alfred Sloan, the supreme architect of the concept, declared that each model 'would attract

> sales from below that price, selling to those customers who might be willing to pay a little more for the additional quality'.

This strategy has long been adopted by Ford and is presently being implemented by Japanese vehicle manufacturers.

Recurring revenue

Recurring revenue is that steady profit stream generated from such products as consumables, disposables, and replacement and short-life items; or from services such as preventative maintenance and updating of software.

In some ways closely allied in concept to repeat sales, such a source of income also depends on taking care of customers for continuance. Many recurring sales ride on the back of the initial sale. For example, a coffee filter machine requires filter papers on a regular basis. It is certainly worthwhile for the manufacturer to consider bringing these profits in-house by manufacturing these ancillaries itself.

There are some significant differences between repeat and recurring revenue, however. Indeed, recurring revenue can often represent an even more significant opportunity for companies. Such income can generate higher margins, often requires considerably less selling effort, and is much more stable in a downturn than repeat sales.

One of the most important advantages of the recurring concept over the repeat concept is that the perception of price is much diminished. A consumer 'big ticket' purchase may require considerable saving. However, an expensive industrial product cannot be easily bought if it does not appear in a budget. But if the product's function can be achieved by a product or a service requiring a small outlay and then regular small payments (perhaps related directly to the use of the product), then both the customer's perceived risk and cash flow are reduced.

Winning such profits does require a detailed understanding of the key success factors, and often considerable up-front work – for example, in product development. The most important recurring revenue strategies will now be considered.

Consumables

Perhaps the first continuing revenue concept that comes to most people's minds, this strategy of building a long-term profit stream while locking out the competition at the same time is very effective. In essence, a product is sold which requires a regular supply of ancillary products which are 'consumed' in the operation of the product. These are the consumables.

Examples of products which generate consumable revenue include vacuum cleaners (paper bags), photocopiers (toner cartridges) and cars (petroleum). Personal planning systems (like Filofax and its many imitators) can generate lucrative consumable income from the inserts which, over their lifetime, can far outweigh the up-front income from the cover.

Spare parts for products can also be seen as consumables, although on a longer time-scale than most consumables. Sales of spares can actually be increased in a downturn by selling the idea that using spares can make machines last longer, that it's cheaper than replacing the whole machine, and that possible cash flow problems caused by a machine being out of action during a long repair could be even more catastrophic in a recession. Indeed, one of the companies that I have worked with was able, by aggressive attention, to raise spares sales revenue by 50 per cent within a short space of time by the use of a telesales campaign to inform customers of the consequences of not having spares to hand.

Perhaps the classic example of a consumable strategy is that of King Gillette, which has ensured the continuing success of the shaving razors which still bear his name. Note particularly the importance of locking in the customer and locking out the competition.

Gillette. King Gillette was not the first person to supply a safety razor, consisting of a handle and replacement blades, to the public. But he was the first to employ the tactic of offering the handle at less than the cost of making it.

At 55 cents, the handle retailed at just a fifth of the manufacturing cost. Into the handle fitted the blades which, at a price of 5 cents each, often gave as many as five or six shaves. Since each blade cost Gillette maybe 1 or 2 cents, he made his profits on the blades.

In comparison, competitors tended to sell their handles for $5 each. To the customer, then, the initial price of Gillette's handle was a tenth of his competitors, which considerably reduced the apparent cost.

Central to the pricing policy was the careful design of the handle so that only Gillette blades could be fitted. When competitors' blades sold for less than 2 cents against Gillette's 5 cents, this strategy was critical in bringing the lucrative consumable revenue to Gillette.

King Gillette also employed the tactic of persuading retailers that it was not in their interests to tie up valuable shelf space with the low price consumables of more than one razor manufacturer. This of course had the effect of reinforcing his efforts to lock out the competition from such a valuable profit stream.

Disposables

Disposable products can be a very effective recurring revenue-producing concept. Like a repeat purchase, when the product's life is over, another is bought. However, the disposable product, because of its short life, typically low price and need for regular replacement, shares many characteristics with those of the consumable product, as the following example illustrates.

> **Bic.** It was not until the 1980s that a major competitor to Gillette's highly successful strategy appeared. In the same way that the safety razor had substituted for the village barber, so it was that the disposable razor usurped the safety razor. The chief rival of Gillette, taking much of its market and spawning dozens of imitators, was Baron Bich, the chairman of Bic. An accomplished expert in the sale of disposable products, Bic employed the same tactics that he had used to great success with disposable ballpens and later cigarette lighters. He recognized that the convergence of new materials, low-cost production techniques and less service-intensive distribution had combined with the emergence of the 'throw-away society' to generate the opportunity for disposable products.

It does seem to be a truism, which consumable revenue specialists should bear in mind, that all products which consist of a product and a related consumable are doomed to be overtaken by a disposable product. The traditional pen, for example, with its need for ink bottles and, later, refill cartridges has given way to the throw-away pen. Many pens today, for which refills used to be sold, are, more often than not, only available as a sealed unit which must be replaced lock, stock and barrel when the ink supply is exhausted.

Interestingly, the emergence of concern over the environment has led to a return to recycling, which can provide opportunities in many spheres for collection, recycling or safe disposal of waste products.

Services

Many services can be offered in such a way as to contribute recurring revenue. Companies offering a product which requires servicing, for example, often sell a contract to supply preventative maintenance after the warranty period has expired, since this provides continuing revenue.

Similar opportunities might include the provision of an updating service for a reference work concerning the influence of the law on business practice, maintenance of a software package as defects are discovered and the client's requirements change, and a news service on developments in a country and their implications.

Basic services and repair are often less sensitive than products to a downturn because they can be hard to put off, are paid for when they are needed, payments are relatively small (and therefore easier for a customer to find), and the results are immediate.

Comparing the revenue earned nationally for housing construction with that for housing maintenance shows up the relative insensitivity of maintenance to a downturn. If your pipes have burst because of cold weather (a common occurrence in the UK where pipes have in the past been placed outside house walls), for example, you are hardly likely to delay calling out a repair person.

More discretionary services could be reduced, however, where the value of the money saved by the customer outweighs the inconvenience of him doing it himself. Where deterioration is not so visible or so immediate in its impact, expenditure is often put off for another day.

Referrals

Referring the customer to another product or service provided by your company leverages each customer to the hilt. Just think, for example, of the last time you visited your local corner-shop or convenience store. Perhaps you went in with the intention of just buying, say, a carton of milk. Yet somehow you came out with a loaf of bread and a newspaper. That's because the storekeeper had leveraged your visit by persuading you to buy other products. He displayed them to you and made the convenience explicit to you, the customer, of having all these products under one roof. Such advantages explain the growth and consolidation of supermarkets and hypermarkets around the world.

Emphasizing to your customers their new-found ability to satisfy their needs in one place is the basis for the construction of the advertising multinationals of the 1980s. They have tended to become 'one-stop shops' in providing market research and media-buying, in addition to the traditional backbone of creative copy.

Some of these groups have combined such a strategy with a coverage of many world markets. Many of these companies have based their growth rationale on the increasing trend of their customers towards global marketing based on the convergence of life-styles in the developed economies. They are therefore selling the convenience to multinationals of being able to visit one location to deal with all their marketing needs for their global campaigns.

The advertising agencies have based their hopes of recouping their acquisition costs of companies offering complementary services by referring customers across subsidiaries. A customer entering the lobby of one company for advertising can then be persuaded to engage the company in some market research first and in purchasing media space at a discount.

The concept of the one-stop shop is particularly important for non-sophisticated buyers, and for buyers for whom the convenience of such a network of bureaux outweighs the possible greater capabilities of specialists. Indeed, therein may lie the limit to growth of these companies as some clients raise questions about the quality of the bureaux in the network and their lack of freedom to use (in their view, perhaps better) outside agencies.

Referring customers to another service provided by your organization has been given an unusual twist by Firestone. Unlike the advertising companies which have historically drawn their business from customers wanting their main-line advertising product, Firestone attempted to generate sales of its tyres through selling an ancillary product. Well aware that customer loyalty in the car tyre market was non-existent, the company decided to build retail outlets offering auto services. The idea was formulated as being 'if you trust a Firestone dealer for service, you'll trust him for tyres'.

Another way of increasing the convenience value of a company is by having tie-ups with other companies. Joint ventures and distributing a complementary product can expand your product range at little extra cost. This has proved an essential strategy for airlines in the US where one of the key advantages of the hub and spoke operations is their ability to 'hold on' to passengers throughout their trip. By using affiliations with other airlines offering complementary routes, and carefully arranging scheduling to minimize passengers' time on the ground, an airline can serve customers on a multiplicity of routes at low cost. The advantage to the customer is that he can arrange with just one airline to fly from A to C via B instead of having to arrange connections with two airlines. This can also be achieved at a much lower price than going from A to C directly.

Partnership

The value-managed relationship

Eventually, the time will come when suppliers will have to address the cost issue directly. It is then that it becomes necessary to shift from the previous ways of differentiating against the competition to helping the customers with their operating costs.

At first sight, the options might seem limited. But there is a solution which provides real opportunity for a supplier. This is the so-called value-managed relationship (VMR) which can give rise to a 'win–win' situation where both parties benefit.

In a partnership between a company and its supplier, a VMR can avoid the normal adversarial attitudes. Its aim is to reduce the overall costs for both parties; that is, to find ways of managing more cost-effectively the 'value chain' – the sequential process in which value is added to a product through the various stages and companies before reaching the final customer.

A VMR is a trusting relationship in which information is shared. The use of lateral thinking from the two disparate viewpoints of supplier and customer can produce some surprisingly large benefits for both parties. Cost savings of 10–15 per cent are quite achievable.

VMRs can substitute for price cuts

By emphasizing quality and service, as well as system economies, a VMR can substitute for price cuts in holding customers. For example, in a manufacturing environment, better information on the partner's production schedules reduces the risks that the other partner must face (from the consequences of late delivery, for instance). This leads to better planning and lower inventory requirements to cover against risk. Hence, a great deal of working capital can be released for better uses. Such benefits can take the pressure off a customer's demand for price cuts in difficult trading conditions.

Such a relationship, with its closely tied information transfer and ways of doing business, can be seen as a form of customization of the product. Therefore, a VMR is both a way of locking in the customer (who would find it hard to find such a product elsewhere) and locking out the competition (since it is difficult to compare costs directly for such a customized product). A product which closely meets the customer's needs will differentiate a supplier from its competitors in the customer's eyes, and this will offset price attractions of other suppliers.

In the longer term, a VMR can provide the supplier with the potential for maintaining price longer in a downturn, and the possibility of premium pricing in an upturn.

VMRs can prevent loss of customers

On account of the investment in time and resources in setting up VMRs, both partners try hard to maintain the relationship even when conditions become difficult. The prospect of setting up a VMR again with another supplier tends to be daunting. Indeed, vehicle component manufacturers who have built up close relationships with motor manufacturers have been gratified to find that their customers are reluctant to sever their relationships in a downturn and look for cheaper products elsewhere. Investment in a VMR can therefore provide stability for both sides.

No better time to set up a VMR

VMRs are easier to set up in difficult trading conditions, when the cost benefits will be particularly welcome. Ordinarily, customers and suppliers tend to be reluctant to share information and to engage in a relationship which may close off some of their options. It is the massive potential for reduced costs which provides the stimulus to set up a VMR, and at no time is this a greater imperative than in a trying economic climate.

There are three key priorities in setting up a VMR.

- The sheer effort in building these long-term relationships forces companies to consolidate around a small number of low-cost suppliers who can supply a high proportion of the companies' needs.
- Since so many benefits are indirect and not easily quantifiable, the focus must be on the whole value chain providing value to the end-customer, and not just on the immediate area of contact between the two parties.
- Then a partner should be trusting enough to delegate as many as possible of the decisions to the supplier, so avoiding undue interference.

So far, a VMR has, been seen as existing solely between a company and its supplier. But a change of viewpoint will indicate that it can be enormously beneficial to extend the VMR further down the chain – from the company to its customer. The same concept can also be exploited to great effect inside the company – between operating units and departments. The examples which follow show the many varieties of possibilities for both partners to benefit from a VMR.

Reduced costs throughout the whole value chain

VMRs allow customers (and yourself) to save money without the expedient of your having to give away profits in the form of reduced prices. A good example is that of Supervalu.

Supervalu, the largest wholesaler to independent grocery retailers in the US, uses VMR to differentiate itself from the competition by adding value to its product and reducing the customer's costs.

Supervalu works with its customers, the grocery stores, from start to finish. It finds the site, designs the store, finances the equipment, sets the shelves, trains the butchers and assistants, plans the premises, writes the advertising, looks after the bookkeeping and takes care of the insurance. Supervalu also helps them with computer models of area, the pricing and the product mix, and supplies experts to optimize the benefits. It is by understanding the customers' needs through total involvement in all activities that Supervalu is able to help customers to reach their potential.

How is Supervalu able to offer lower real costs to the customer? Being sole supplier to its retailers, the indirect costs of all these activities are spread over many products; that is, the 'economies of scale' are optimum, reducing costs to a minimum. The company is also non-unionized. These lower costs mean Supervalu can offer additional services to its customers for no extra cost.

Supervalu provides retailers with products at low prices and up-to-date stores with sophisticated operating systems in good locations. The result is that its more than 2000 affiliated stores, handling a total revenue in excess of $5 billion, have achieved 1.5–3 per cent net profit after taxes, far above the industry average of 1 per cent at that time. Supervalu has built a business which provides a lifeline to independent grocery retailers in their battles against the hypermarkets by reducing the effective costs of its customers.

Saving the customer money and inconvenience

One of the most effective ways of getting customer approval is to do for the customer what would be far too costly to do for himself. One such company is Anixter, one of the largest distributors of electrical wire and cable in the US. Realizing that customers 'bought their products by the mile, but used them by the foot', therefore piling up expensive inventory that could quickly become outmoded, Anixter came up with the idea of 'use our inventory: it's better than your cash' by cutting cable to the lengths required by the customer.

Another interesting example is the German **Zeppelin** company. This manufacturer of heavy machinery has set up a database of the maintenance status of its customers' machines. Zeppelin earns a recurring revenue from the planned maintenance while the customers suffer far fewer costly breakdowns, and do not have the inconvenience of systematically monitoring their machines.

Computers provide the key

Many VMRs are made possible only by the advent of affordable computer technology providing a common information database which can be used to coordinate the activity between supplier and customer. However, a survey of over 200 US and UK 'blue chip' companies found that only a tiny handful used their information technology to even a fraction of its potential. The companies described here demonstrate proven ways in which you can use computers for real competitive advantage.

Making it easy for the customer to specify your product

The computer can help the customer by communicating information on the use of your company's product, by supplying essential data which makes the process of selection less painful, and by using its calculation capabilities to find the optimum solution for the customer's problem. These three techniques are illustrated by the following three examples.

ICI agrochemicals. ICI, the large UK chemical combine, has a plant protection division whose computer system was initially set up to allow the company's independent distributors to check inventory levels while out of the office. The advent of the 'Wheat Counsellor' program led to the computer system becoming an information service for the farmers themselves, advising them of the right choice of fungicide for a particular pest and soil combination. For ICI, the system has 'improved farmers' awareness of products', reports the manager in charge, 'as well as raising the support profile of ICI in the distributors' eyes'. Such differentiation has had the added benefit that ICI has 'kept the competition away from this area'.

RibaCad. Placing products in front of the customer and making it simple to select them is the novel idea of the UK's Royal Institution of British Architects, under whose auspices the RibaCad database is marketed. This library holds the computer-aided design specifications of common products, such as door handles, which may be 'injected' into architectural drawings without the need for redrawing.

A survey of architects on product choice revealed that well over half would be influenced if they were to see a drawing of the product at the specifying stage. Suppliers recognize the enormous opportunities offered by this database, as can be seen by the large fees they are willing to pay for their products to be included on the database.

Commercial Union, a leading British insurer, is one of many companies which have set up computer systems to provide on-line quotation information to its intermediaries. The latter are now able to select the best option for a customer's circumstances and calculate the monthly customer payments while the customer waits. The corporation now issues more than four times as many policies for each member of staff, just ten years after its introduction. For an insurer who is critically dependent on the intermediary for market share, the system makes the broker more effective and builds his loyalty.

Rapid transfer of information

VMRs, like successful marriages, are partnerships which depend on open and frequent communication. Clearly, computers hold a key role in collecting the information, and are being used more and more to effect the paperless transfer of information between parties. Courtaulds, a leading clothing and textile company in the UK, has discovered many benefits.

Courtaulds, in the old days, turned to the humble motorcycle courier to transfer computer instructions printed on paper from its main customer clothing retailer Marks & Spencer. Today, orders and instructions are transferred electronically. Courtaulds's contract apparel group can now supply product precisely on time when the retailer needs it. 'It has enabled us to take critical hours out of a very tight schedule', declared an M&S spokesman. In addition, Courtaulds has managed to make the substantial annual saving of a quarter of a million pounds by not needing to employ motorcycle couriers.

Directly linked data networks of cables are a solution to the paperless information transfer problem. But they can be inflexible and expensive. An alternative which is growing in use, and which is specific to two companies, is the electronic clearing house. These systems, such as the well-known Tradanet or Edict networks, avoid the necessity of compatibility of company computers, which has always been the bugbear of computer-based systems. Users range from vehicle to food manufacturers.

The Rover Group of UK motor companies uses such a network to link to Rockwell, an auto-parts manufacturer, to enable the just-in-time ordering so critical in any motor manufacturer's success.

Nestle Rowntree and Reckitt & Colman have employed Tradanet to exchange orders, invoices and delivery notes with the main retailers such as Sainsbury's, the leader in the field. Users report that sales improve because ordering is so much easier for customers. Indeed, one company found the network had helped to win 24 per cent greater sales.

The ultimate is of course electronic point-of-sale updating of inventory and reordering of merchandise. Perhaps the best-known exponent of this strategy is Benetton.

Benetton, the Italian manufacturer and retailer of vibrantly dyed fashion clothing, collects information electronically from each of its shops every day. This information is used to order more inventory for the boutiques from the warehouses, and to change the product mix in production daily. The data on the day's sales, reaching the company's central factory in Italy that evening, is analyzed to determine the changing trends of consumer demand. For example, pullovers, made from wool, are stored in a grey state. If the data shows that red is particularly popular, then the percentage of red pullovers is increased.

Benetton has managed to create real competitive advantage in building an integrated company through understanding the power of rapid transfer of information.

Helping to manage a customer's inventory

VMRs can improve a supplier's forecasting accuracy, helping him to reduce his risk and costs. They aid his planning of capital expenditure. American Hospital Supply is a good example of a company which provides such good value to its customers that they feel no reason to go to competitors.

American Hospital Supply (AHS) has built an unusually strong relationship with the hospitals it supplies with products ranging from drugs to surgical gloves.

By installing thousands of computer terminals in hospitals throughout the country, the company has provided a direct link to its warehouses. This significantly streamlines hospitals' purchases of supplies.

For the hospital, there are three main advantages: lower costs of distribution, easier payment and the convenience of being able to buy most supplies in one place. These are certainly powerful reasons for adopting the AHS system, as we shall see.

'Studies have shown', reports AHS, 'that for every dollar a hospital spends to purchase supplies, it spends another dollar getting them to the doctors and nurses who use them. A large part of that second dollar is the cost of carrying inventory.' AHS holds the inventory, significantly reducing the cost to the hospital. Typical savings have been shown to be 20 per cent of a hospital's purchase costs within one year.

The computer system has many advantages over the previous cumbersome paper system. It is significantly cheaper to maintain critical inventory levels, allows much faster response and delivery, and greatly simplifies the payment process. AHS has claimed that 95 per cent of orders are shipped on the same day.

AHS believes it can provide more than 60 per cent of a hospital's requirements – which means all the convenience to the hospital of a 'one-stop shop'. Lower indirect costs can therefore result from the concomitant savings in purchasing and administration personnel.

For AHS, automated purchasing means the hospitals are tied to a long-term relationship, locking out the competition. In addition, because the prices do not appear on the screen, margins can be higher because it is likely that product prices are not even considered by purchasers. AHS can also benefit from 'economies of scale' when the number of items per order attains a declared 5.8 compared to the industry average of 1.7.

AHS has clearly found its niche in supplying a major service to hospitals. It has reaped a significant reward. With margins at four times the industry average, at one time its annual growth over the five-year period after introduction averaged a phenomenal 17 per cent per year, and the company's market share nudged 50 per cent.

Unichem. Following the example of companies such as McKesson in the US, pharmacies in the UK are now able to order new stock electronically. Indeed, the leading independent pharmaceutical distributor, Unichem, claims that almost all of its orders are paperless. Able to deliver up to twice a day if necessary, the system allows the drugstores to have their inventory managed by Unichem. 'Ultimately', says David Walker, Unichem's management services director,'we'll be able to anticipate what pharmacies want.' In return, Unichem is convinced that 'once committed, a customer is more likely to put most of his business with us'.

Locking in the customer

The computer in a VMR can be an important competitive tool to lock in the customer and lock out the competition. The partnership provides so many benefits and is managed so well that the customer would not want to look elsewhere. By gaining a dominant market share early and increasing investment to improve services to the customer, barriers to entry are raised which may lock out competitors. American Airlines' Sabre airline computer reservation system is perhaps the archetypal example.

American Airlines was in trouble during the early days of the deregulation of US airline routes in the early 1980s because of its old fleet and high labour costs. Recognition that new computer technology could be as important to marketing – through automated reservations and seat control – as investment in new aircraft led to the Sabre computer reservation system becoming an integral part of American's marketing strategy. Sabre was to become a significant factor in the revival of American Airlines in the early 1980s.

By distributing its computer terminals to travel agents over the US, Sabre is now the dominant airline seat distribution network in the US, representing 38 per cent of all the terminals installed. Sabre thus places its name in front of more travel agents than any other, making bookings quick and easy.

With good representation in travel agencies, the ability to offer selective discounts to clear surplus seat capacity and for frequent flier programmes has clearly had a great impact on the company's marketing and economics.

In the competitive environment, it has caused a sea change. Deregulation has tended to help small carriers but has forced them to seek affiliations with bigger carriers which can offer them expertise, stability and, critically, an entry on the display of a travel agent's reservation screen. Indeed, profits from the entry fees on to Sabre have at times earned more profit than its passenger transportation business, and can be used to expand American's activities elsewhere. Sabre has become a vital competitive advantage for American Airlines.

Managing value can avoid price cuts

The costs to a customer of using your product are in fact significantly greater than the initial purchase price. There are downstream costs associated with using your product inside his company. It is by reducing these costs through a form of VMR that a supplier can reduce the pressure exerted on him by the customer to lower his prices. Just such a situation is illustrated by the initiative of a salesman of paint additives.

Paint additive salesman. Faced with a demand for a lower price from an important customer, the salesman had run out of marketing arguments and was under severe pressure to lower his price. By thinking laterally, he was able to come up with an innovative solution which managed to save the customer money yet avoided his having to make price concessions.

Buying time, he was able to discover that the speed of his customer's production processes was limited by certain qualities of his product. He therefore investigated how the additive was used in the customer's plant, and how the product was produced in his company's factory. After carrying out tests, he was able to persuade his production director to make some minor changes to the manufacturing process at minimal cost. The salesman showed that the modified product would allow his customer to increase the speed of his production line by 8 per cent. To the customer, this represented an enormous reduction in the manufacturing cost of his final product: so much so that it was equivalent to a 25–30 per cent reduction in the cost of the salesman's additive.

By concentrating on the value generated by the product, the salesman helped the customer to increase his profit significantly while the salesman was able to overcome pressure to reduce the price of his product.

Appreciating how customers actually use your product or service has remained a much underused practice in the UK. More should follow the example of TV component manufacturers.

TV component manufacturers. It was only when Japanese TV manufacturers came to the UK to set up their European operations and complained about the failure rate of the British-supplied components that component suppliers took an active approach to improving the situation. They were invited to visit the plants of their Japanese customers. Only by really understanding what happened on the assembly floors of the TV manufacturers could the components be properly designed to meet the requirements, with spectacular results. At a then Thorn EMI–Ferguson plant such a reduction in component failures led to an 86 per cent decrease in final assembly rejects within the first year.

Cooperation not confrontation

An extraordinary example of the success of reversing the combative attitudes in a traditional customer–supplier relationship is that of the textile companies of Prato. In the decade after 1970 the production of textiles in the Prato area of Italy doubled while that of the rest of Europe declined steeply. This unexpected success came from an unusual cooperation between a group of Italian textile companies. An independent 'master broker' controls the distribution of work to the cooperating companies, ensuring an equitable sharing. By being close to the market, he is able to disseminate his knowledge of market trends throughout the group, so that all work together to prepare for the next season. Competition problems are overcome in a cooperative manner: if a weaver has guessed wrong on a style one year, another will give him overload work.

Cooperation in such partnerships can provide benefits for all parties.

Working with suppliers to improve the product

So far, we have mainly looked at partnerships with customers. The idea can of course be extended in the other direction, to suppliers. Nissan Motor Manufacturing, Marks & Spencer and Jaguar demonstrate the potential for improving their product by working closely with suppliers.

Nissan Motor Manufacturing UK. The Japanese are well known for their partnerships with their suppliers. But the widespread belief that the different trading conditions in the West mean that ideas cannot be easily transferred can be countered by the success of Japanese companies in the UK. Holding the bulk of Japanese investment in Europe, the UK plays host to over 600 Japanese companies. One of these is Nissan Motor Manufacturing UK, which has had great success in fostering relationships with its suppliers.

A 'Supply Development Team' of senior managers trained in the UK, Japan and the US was established, committed to improving suppliers' performance. An initial period of several intensive weeks with each supplier suffices to transfer new techniques for improvement. The suppliers, at first guarded, have overwhelmed the company with their enthusiasm. This, and the increasing UK parts content of Nissan's cars, demonstrates the worth of the programme.

Ian Gibson, chief executive, believes that much of the dramatic change undergone throughout the UK motor industry in the 1980s has been due to the example of Nissan: 'People realize that they have no excuse any more. You can say to yourself, what works on the far side of the world won't work here. It's a bit difficult to say, what works on the other side of the river won't work here. It concentrates the mind.'

Marks & Spencer, one of the leading clothing and food retailers in the UK, is well known for supplying quality goods at affordable prices through its close links with suppliers.

Marks & Spencer. Since the opening of its own textile laboratories and 'Merchandise Development Department' in the 1930s, the company has advised and coaxed its suppliers to modernize. By closely following improvements in machinery, processes and fibres, the company's technologists can prod manufacturers to continue to reduce costs and to increase quality.

At the same time, the closeness of the buying departments with the technologists enables the supplier to supply the merchandise which the public requires, and to meet variations in demand with the minimum of waste. That this is a close partnership is highlighted by Marcus Sieff who, as erstwhile chairman, was concerned at a decline in the company's shoe sales. The suppliers felt that the styles were old-fashioned and, after some reluctance, told him so. Sieff listened to their advice, changed the senior managers in the shoe department and reported that shoe sales 'improved dramatically'.

A much reduced time-to-market for new textile fibres, finishes and fashions, customized to M&S's customers' requirements, is a further benefit. Its well-managed relationships with its suppliers have long been recognized as a key source of competitive advantage for M&S.

Working with its suppliers remains an important factor in both cost reduction and quality improvement for Jaguar.

Jaguar. As part of its renaissance in the 1980s, Jaguar surveyed BMW, Mercedes-Benz and its own customers in order to discover how the quality standards and warranty statistics compared. Jaguar was able to isolate 150 important faults in their cars, 60 per cent of which were due to supplies of substandard components. Patiently explaining to the suppliers the cost and importance of fixing these faults, Jaguar provided technical assistance to suppliers to raise their quality standards. Where necessary, additional pressure was exerted by refusing to sign contracts unless suppliers agreed to pay all Jaguar's warranty costs if their product failed.

Internal partnerships pay dividends too

The advantages of a VMR need not be restricted to managing the value of a product transferred between the two companies. They also apply to processes requiring the involvement of two or more departments or activities. When one area's problem affects another, there is an opportunity for a cooperative form of internal partnership. Toyota's well-known technique of laying the responsibility for the quality of a piece of work on the last person to handle it ensures that each person must work closely with another to meet his quality standard. In this way concern over the quality of the final output pervades throughout the company. This internal partnership of workers has provided the basis of Toyota's world standing.

Nucor, the highly successful US steel milling company, has managed to remove 10 per cent or more from the cost base of a traditional steel supplier. One of the ways it has managed to do this is by rethinking the handling of product from one activity to another. Engineers found that they could avoid the conventional process where the steel is allowed to cool between rolling stages and needs to be reheated. By passing hot steel directly from one stage to another, the company was able to save the cost of a great deal of energy. So by managing its own value chain better, Nucor brought its cost base under those of the behemoths of the industry despite their greater economies of scale.

Existing customers are important to a company. They need to be satisfied and nurtured to ensure a continuing revenue stream. Managing value for both parties is the basis for long-lasting and highly beneficial partnerships.

Chapter 8

Winning Revenue from New Customers

Relationships unfreeze

In difficult times the previously cosy relationships between customers and their suppliers unfreeze under pressure. Customers begin to look hard at what their supplier is offering them. It is then that go-getting companies can see an opportunity to win business in the short term and to build a strong relationship which will lock the customer into them long into the upturn.

Competition then becomes fierce as each company tries to build or maintain its share in a stagnant market. Hence, additional markets where products can be sold provide a welcome respite from the competition, and give the opportunity to build cash flow, profits and market share.

Old ways aren't working and customers are looking for better ways. New products and approaches which provide better value to the customer can persuade potential customers to buy from you. Since pressure from competitors is minimized by circumventing them with new products and ideas, margins are often higher, too.

This chapter suggests where the new customer can be seen as a rich vein to be mined. These fall into three logical categories. One way of selling more product is to escape existing competitive pressures and to sell to new customers. Then there are new ways to reach potential customers more cost effectively. Finally, since the old ways aren't working, you can deflect competition by selling new products.

When conditions become difficult it is easy to retreat into the familiar. Salespeople call on their existing customers far too often in order to escape from the harsh realities of life. New customers are there for the taking and this chapter will demonstrate ways of exploiting the opportunity.

Find new customers

Product coverage, presence and hit rate

In winning new sales it is particularly important to maximize the segments of the market you can address. This is largely governed by product coverage and presence.

Product coverage is the percentage of the market that a company's product can address. For example, if half of the market requires a certain type of packaging and your product is not made that way, your product can only cover a maximum of 50 per cent of the market. Hence an important opportunity to increase your wins of new customers, in this case, would be to sell the product in the packaging required by the other half of the market.

Product presence denotes what percentage of the outlet channels your product can be sold in. For example, if a survey shows that 30 per cent of the potential customers of your product buy from a distribution outlet you do not serve, your product presence cannot be more than 70 per cent. Hence, more product could be sold by serving additional distribution channels. Several capital equipment manufacturers, for instance, have won more business by expanding their distribution to serve original equipment manufacturers, and by having their products incorporated into the customers' products.

Finally, there is the hit rate, or the percentage of the time that your product wins the sale when the customer is faced with your product and its competitors. Since direct competition and alternative substitutes exist for every product, a product's hit rate is improved by targeting product markets where competition is less fierce. That these exist, and can be taken advantage of, is shown by the examples which follow.

The principles of product coverage, presence and hit rate are central to any strategy of increasing sales.

Hit 'em where they ain't

'You can be sure of succeeding in your attacks', wrote the Chinese strategist Sun Tzu, 'if you only attack places which are undefended.'

The hit rate and the degree of pricing freedom open to any supplier depend on both the product's perceived value to the customer and the competitive intensity of the market. So if a company can usefully avoid competition then it should do so. Honeywell, the computer and automated controls manufacturer, for example, has in the past made a deliberate point of targeting more rural cities to avoid competing with IBM, which is particularly strong in bigger, more urban cities. Colgate has employed a similar strategy.

> **Colgate.** In 1971, Colgate was underdog to Procter & Gamble (P&G) in about half of its business. Since P&G was considerably bigger, Colgate's margins were being held down by P&G's presence. Colgate therefore devised the strategy of expanding operations abroad, where P&G was not so strong. By 1976, three-quarters of Colgate's business was either comfortably placed against P&G or didn't face it at all.

If the competitors are not meeting the real needs of customers in some sectors, then companies can address these markets with a better product and meet unsatisfied demand and low competition. This is plainly happening in the vehicle market where Japanese and German cars have vastly expanded their market share in the US against the domestic suppliers because they have covered market needs not being served by the leaders.

Similarly, Miller moved from seventh place in the US beer market to a close second by developing a segment not exploited by others – that of light beer – and which has remained one of the fastest growing segments for some time.

Flanking attacks like these on competitors have historically offered a much higher success than head-on attacks. Indeed, Liddell Hart, the military historian, analyzed the 30 most important conflicts up to the First World War – almost 300 campaigns – and found that only six battles had achieved decisive results from frontal attacks.

Go for the big potential customers

If the sales in the industry have traditionally come from a large number of small customers, then it is wise to attack a few selected potential customers, each capable of producing volume business fast. Although the smaller customers may be useful for the long term, it is more realistic to hope for rapid growth by going for the bigger potential customers. More ideas can be gleaned from the section 'Go where the money is' in the previous chapter.

Target insensitive sectors

Customers whose spending is sheltered from the winds of change naturally represent a prime target for marketing. Maytag, the number one in white goods in the US, appreciates them. It sells the most expensive range of washing machines in the US, with top ratings in *Consumer Reports* (the equivalent of the UK's *Which?* magazine). Being premium products, they are aimed at the replacement market rather than the more cyclical first-time market. 'Often we don't get the first-time buyer, but we get the second-time buyer', said the president. They're going to buy in a downturn because, 'after all, you're not going to leave your washing around in a big bundle on the floor'.

Seeing which sectors have been sensitive in the past can be instructive. Does the industry have a history of market share changes occurring during similar times? It has been shown, for instance, that in economic recession in the US the relatively upmarket department store Sears tends to lose share to the more downmarket K-Mart and JC Penney, as consumers shop around for the lower-priced deals. Speciality retailers like Liz Claiborne and The Limited in the US showed increased earnings in 1990 while recession took its toll of department stores.

The must-have categories

Then there are the 'must-have' categories – medical insurance, fire insurance, computer support, etc. In these dangerous times, suppliers declare, such disasters could lead to a major unplanned cash-flow problem which might cause the downfall of the entire company.

Pharmaceuticals are well known as being insensitive to recession. If a customer is ill, for example, getting better will be his first concern. Ciba-Geigy provides the example.

> **Ciba-Geigy** is a Swiss chemical company which, with half its product mix being drugs and the other half being high margin agrochemicals, managed to increase its profits in a recessionary period. By contrast, all its more industrially based competitors suffered only declining profits. Over 1980–82, Ciba-Geigy increased its revenue by 16 per cent while its profits grew by 100 per cent. Conversely, Du Pont was down 44 per cent, Hoechst down 43 per cent, and Bayer 78 per cent.
>
> Ciba-Geigy owes much of its resilience to its carefully targeted product sectors.

Some segments of the media market remain relatively untouched since people's need for information remains important. However, discretionary items, such as expensive non-news magazines, have been seen to suffer greatly.

Food is often thought to be insensitive to difficult times. 'Everyone has to eat', the stock analysts say. But margins come under pressure and sales of high-price speciality items are likely to diminish. During boom years, food retailers are under pressure from their investors to produce higher margins, and so their product mix moves towards speciality goods of higher quality. Yet in a downturn, these retailers are often caught on the hop as the consumers' need to reduce expenditure moves their purchases downmarket.

This becomes apparent when the market shares of low-price stores are compared to those of the others. The dramatic cuts in the prices of food in leading supermarkets in the UK in the 1990s recession (led by one of the leading stores, Tesco's, with a 50 per cent drop in price in August 1991 for some of its own-label products), and the entering into the UK market of the ultra-low-price German retail chain Aldi, highlight the fallacy of thinking that the entire food market is insensitive.

In all markets it is necessary to look carefully at the data to avoid missing out on opportunities because of too wide ranging a generalization. An interesting study in sensitivity to recession is the quoted UK company of BET.

BET is a company built on the foundation of providing support services to businesses, with the slogan of 'you look after the core businesses, we'll take care of the chore businesses'. A series of acquisitions and divestments over a period of ten years was employed by the former chief executive, Nicholas Wills, to make the company 'recession-resistant'. However, the advent of recessionary conditions brought 'that awful phrase' (to use his own words) back to haunt him.

A decline of 33 per cent in annual profits in 1990–91 was blamed on rising interest costs (which doubled the charges on the company to over a third of profits) and recessionary conditions in its principal markets. Examining the figures more closely shows that, while much of the strategy held up, a misunderstanding of the market led to the poor performance.

The bulk of BET's operating profits came from its Initial subsidiary which supplies towels and hand dryers for companies' wash-rooms. Revenues held up well, with some gain coming from cross-selling of other services to existing customers. Some decline in margins was experienced. Companies supplying security services and products 'performed relatively well'. Clearly, BET had successfully targeted some insensitive sectors.

Companies offering crane and scaffolding hire suffered very predictably as new construction nosedived in the recession. However, industry analysts and BET management were shocked by the two-thirds reduction in operating profits for the property improvement services division. How could this occur to a division in a supposedly recession-resistant company?

While industry statistics do indicate the overall activity in maintenance services to the building and housing sector to be relatively insensitive to recession compared to building construction, this does remain a highly fragmented market with low barriers to entry and questionable economies of scale. Smaller competitors were thus able to offer cut-price contracts without having to pay the high overheads of BET. It seemed then that BET had misinterpreted the industry situation.

While some of BET's strategy held up, misinterpretation of the market environment prevented it from reaching its full potential.

Counter-cyclicality

One way to take advantage of a downturn is to retarget the company towards a segment which is growing when neighbouring segments are falling. To do this, it is necessary to disaggregate the data and look for the niches underneath. For example, even while the whole population is decreasing (as is the case in much of the West), it is well known that the number and proportion of over-55s is increasing. Targeting their needs can provide a great opportunity. So even while the whole market is going down, there may be parts going up.

The dream of a company in pain in a downturn is to have a cash cow which holds up profits because its market demand increases when other businesses are down. However, this leads to a diversified company with all the difficulties of management which that implies.

Diversity

Serving a diversity of sectors can ensure a good weighting of profits in sectors less affected by the downturn. Diversity therefore can help to protect profits in economic downturns. General Electric in the US, for example, had by 1981 managed to record 26 straight quarters of improved results through two and a half recessions because of the diversity of its product base. However, diversity has made the company hard for investors to understand, which is one reason the company's stock has historically traded at a discount to its sector.

Companies sometimes diversify into sectors which they believe to be counter-cyclical. Few of these companies are successful because they misinterpret the market environment, and where they hoped to have at least one company generating cash at one time they may find both consuming cash. An apparent exception is USX which deliberately diversified in 1982 away from its original US Steel base into energy since the two sectors had proved counter-cyclical in the past. So far it has continued to work: when steel profits are down, energy profits are up, and vice versa. However, such diversity also prevents the stock price from taking off when times are good since the overall growth of the company is lower at any one time than the separate businesses alone.

One problem to avoid is falling foul of the temptation to acquire unrelated businesses as part of the company's portfolio. A study by Michael Porter, published in the *Harvard Business Review* [4], found that the success rate of unrelated acquisitions was under 25 per cent.

Niche vs bulk products

In markets where there is overcapacity and you cannot become the lowest cost producer, it makes sense to find a way of differentiating your product.

Moving to serve niches with speciality products may provide more stable demand and higher margins. ICI provides a well-known demonstration.

> **ICI**, the world's fourth largest chemicals group, suffered greatly in the UK recession in the early 1980s. In the five years following, the company came to direct more resources towards the low-volume, high-price speciality parts of the chemical industry, such as pharmaceuticals, agrochemicals and paints. Apparently, this policy had not gone far enough – for the next recession again impacted profits severely: down 21 per cent.
>
> The reduction in profits was especially steep in many of ICI's bulk chemicals businesses, such as petrochemicals, plastics and general industrial materials, which are sold at low prices and in high volumes. As these are segments of the industry which generate large profits in an upswing, the management was clearly reluctant to emasculate an important future profit source.
>
> It appears then that ICI's general policy of moving out of bulk products was justified, although one might perhaps argue it was not carried through far enough.

For some companies, their niche has become their tomb. Non-essential products whose functional purpose can be achieved at much lower price from a competing source are clearly vulnerable in a downturn. Opportunities lie elsewhere.

Public sector contracts

There are four possible sectors from which new revenue can come: business, the consumer, the government and export.

Some government contracts can provide a stable source of business. They are often long term, and inflation adjustments, escalation clauses and sometimes cost-plus contracts can be negotiated. Government contracts are often of the 'must-have' category, and reneging on such contracts can be politically damaging.

Defence has been the archetypal government contract since the start of the Cold War. But the advent of 'glasnost' and 'perestroika' has exposed this safe haven to turbulent winds of change. Rolls-Royce aero-engines, for example, suffered from economic recession in the early 1990s in several important Western markets coupled with a downturn in defence spending. Profits declined by 24 per cent. 'In the early 1980s the civil engine business fell but the defence business remained strong', declared the chief executive. 'Now both sides are down.'

Disadvantages of public sector contracts are the long lead time between enquiry and order, and a possible politically induced programme-stretching or moratorium.

Exploit brand name insensitivity

In a recession, markets tend to become polarized between generics (cheap, no-nonsense products under the retailer's brand name) and stand-alone brand names. The products in the middle are often badly squeezed by the low price of the basic generics, and the strength of the brand names.

Sony, Mercedes-Benz and Guinness possess well-known brands and are able to appreciate the insensitivity of brand names to a downturn. Akio Morita, chairman of Sony, remarked that: 'Sony sells to middle class consumers. It's like Mercedes, it's the last to suffer in a recession.' Their discretionary income is less sensitive than others, and a brand name's power is in its perceived 'must-have' quality. Indeed, when we look at Mercedes-Benz, we find that top-of-the-range cars have consistently had waiting lists of months for some models throughout recession years. Yet it was companies such as Volkswagen who were laying off workers. Guinness has exploited this effect to the maximum.

> **Guinness**, the company which owns the Johnny Walker whisky brand and which produces some 40 per cent of all Scotch whisky, emphasized to its shareholders in 1990 that customers were continuing to trade up to its more profitable premium and de-luxe brands. By dint of effort of its marketing teams, the company reported that de-luxe spirits volumes had increased 4 per cent in the UK and the Irish Republic in a market that had, overall, fallen by the same amount. Published figures from Guinness's subsidiary distillers show that a 1 per cent shift in volume from cheap bulk whisky to de-luxe brands can add as much as 9 per cent to profits. Such is the potential of brand names.

Companies should examine their product range and their markets to find softer parts of the market to attack, and to exploit those products in their ranges which will remain firmer on price.

Legislation and the environment

Since legislation requires some time to produce and implement, it can be the case that new laws come into effect just when a company's demand is falling off due to the difficult business environment. The need to comply can provide valuable sales to such companies, and can make customers very insensitive to price. Customers often ignore even far-reaching regulations until the last possible moment, which provides a very rapid build-up of income.

The growing awareness of the need to protect the environment and public health can also provide real opportunities.

I challenge anyone to produce a company more insensitive to downturns than Domino Printing Sciences plc. It is a company which has not only been able to exploit new legislation to good effect, but has also maximized the stability of its profits through a variety of approaches. A textbook example.

> **Domino Printing Sciences plc** designs, manufactures and markets ink-jet printers which typically place date and batch codes on products. The company's main market segments, representing some three-quarters of its business, are food and pharmaceuticals, which are relatively stable in downturns. The company's sales figures were improved by the vast expansion in demand for its product caused by the introduction of wider health legislation. In addition, with 80 per cent of its revenue deriving from overseas markets, this UK-based company was relatively isolated from the economic downturn in its home market in the early 1990s. The company's sales in many of its non-UK markets experienced high growth rates: 40 per cent in the Middle East and 19 per cent in the US. Stability was further ensured by its high proportion of repeat sales and its substantial recurring revenue from consumables, spares and service (which generated some 40 per cent of the company's profits).
>
> It should therefore come as no surprise to find that the company, with a high market share, a well-recognized brand name and a reputation for reliability, reported a profit increase of 44 per cent in 1991 in the midst of a recession. By targeting insensitive sectors and countries, taking advantage of new legislation, and maximizing continuing revenue, such a company deserves the title of the most recession-insensitive company.

Dual marketing

Dual marketing is an example of increasing product presence; that is, using several channels to distribute essentially the same product. Not only does this increase exposure to new customers, but it can also help to reduce sensitivity to a downturn. If the demand in one sector is down, for instance, then companies may be able to distribute more product through another channel.

Apple Computers, for example, retargeted its original home-use focus to the business customer for whom the products represent greater value and who can afford them. However, Apple continues to sell to its well-enfranchised consumers in a dual marketing strategy.

Industrial sectors tend to have longer purchasing cycles. As many corporate customers eventually supply consumers and are farther up the chain from the consumer-in-the-street, decisions suffer from a time-lag, which means that business sales tend to hold up for some while after that of the consumer. Unfortunately, margins can differ substantially, which often leads companies like Dana Corporation to consider dual marketing to both industrial and consumer sectors. This large US auto parts concern had a choice about the focus of its sales. Should it continue to supply Ford in an OEM (original equipment manufacturer) relationship, or should it move to selling to consumers?

Ford at that time was putting suppliers under pressure by offering long-term contracts only to those companies who strove for productivity improvements of 8 per cent per annum or more. The consumer aftermarket, however, was under much less pressure.

Indeed, it was found that manufacturers of power transmission drives could charge consumer end-users 25 per cent more than they could OEMs because the replacement part is of more value to the end-user – the OEM would see it as a major cost of the machine. These are typical considerations in a dual marketing strategy.

Exploit time-lags

Some sectors and geographical areas lag or lead the downturn seen in other sectors. Companies which can switch to sell to those areas or can raise the proportion of business from those sectors can reap benefits.

As an example, consider the housing market in the UK. During the 1980s, wages and salaries increased in the South-East far faster than in the North on the back of shortages of skilled people. The housing market in the South boomed, with people taking on enormous mortgages, some accepting a lower disposable income than in the North. Further skill shortages in the South and better communications and cheaper housing in the North led to a northerly ripple of rises in wages and house prices. But when interest rates almost doubled at the end of the 1990s, the southern housing market plummeted. However, the northern housing market continued to see increased prices for over one and a half years afterwards. Builders able to move a greater proportion of their work to the North could maintain good performance longer and exploit the time lag.

Changing the geographic focus

Using the same product abroad can save having to alter the product. You can exploit a localized recession in your main market area by entering foreign markets or increasing your non-domestic sales. If that region or country is still growing, and your moves are not aggressive, you may find your competition less fierce. Companies like Fluke and UK steel makers have made this strategy pay off.

Fluke is the third largest US manufacturer in electronic test and measuring equipment. Due to a large proportion of foreign sales, the company weathered an industry recession in 1984 in remarkably good shape. At the end, revenues were up 4 per cent on the previous year to $217 million despite a decrease of 20 per cent in domestic sales. This result was entirely due to foreign sales which represented 37 per cent of the company's total revenue.

UK steel makers. Exports allowed the UK's small independent steel makers to protect themselves from a 6 per cent drop in the home market in 1989–90 by a 33 per cent rise in export sales, giving them a small rise in revenues for the year. 'If it were not for exports', said a director of a local employers' federation, 'life would have been much more difficult.'

For UK machine tools, the picture was similar. At one time in the recession of the early 1990s, it was reported that machine-tool orders in the UK were almost a fifth down on the year before, yet export orders were almost a third up.

If a region is growing and others are still in recession, the cash flow from that region can be used to take advantage of opportunities in recession-hit regions. For instance, when a pronounced slump in the UK construction industry began in the late 1980s, several French companies crossed the English Channel to buy up some of those companies in the sector.

When the international gases company BOC took over Airco in the US, the combined company's performance during the first few years (1979 and 1980) was buoyed up by the company's strong advance in Australia and South Africa, whose economies have in the past habitually lagged world trends.

The situation has changed now: Australia was in the depths of a recession in the early 1990s along with the economies of the English-speaking world, whereas Japan stood out as being an unusual market in that it has slow-downs but rarely downturns. The economy and corporate cash flow just seem to keep on growing with barely a hiccup. In the 20 years before the 1990s the Japanese economy has dropped into negative real growth only once, and in all but two of these years it grew more than 5 per cent in real terms.

The greater interdependence of economies today has reduced the potential for such an export strategy. John Young, chief executive officer of Hewlett-Packard, reported that while overseas markets had grown faster than the domestic market for many of his products for several years, and had grown to represent 55 per cent of sales, these foreign markets had 'slowed down dramatically' in the recessions of the early 1990s.

There are also difficulties with ramping up sales effort at the last moment. Exporting, unless of a commodity product sold with marginal pricing to off-load capacity, may require a longer-term effort to provide the most of the opportunity.

Offsetting sluggish domestic sales by swiftly switching to exports is very difficult unless a company has the foundation of healthy margins.

Considerably greater costs can be generated by going for export orders. Air fares, hotel bills, car rentals and advisers are the most immediate expenses. It also requires significant management time – a penalty which must also be allowed for.

Far from improving a company's position in the short term, export sales attempts could worsen it. For some companies, 'it takes 18 months to seal a contract', declares truckmaker Leyland Daf, and 'in the short term it would make a marginal contribution'. This is echoed by British Steel where an export manager warned: 'Exporting is very complex, costly, and risky. It is easy to get caught. It is not a panacea. Off-loading spare capacity is not the same as an export strategy.' Companies therefore have to be well prepared to take advantage of growth in foreign markets when their home markets are down. The usual attitude is that it is necessary to cut back to improve the core business before thinking of expanding overseas.

However, the opportunities are there for those willing to prepare beforehand, as exemplified by Baker Perkins. A bread-making equipment manufacturer in the UK, the company derives some 80 per cent of its revenue from non-UK sales. 'Exports', reported a company spokesman, 'have carried the company through the latest recession.'

Selling to Third World countries has long been an outlet for Western companies. The sharp drop in home demand and the difficulties experienced in selling to other sophisticated Western nations, which tend to remain loyal to their existing suppliers, can provide real opportunities.

'Export or die!', shout companies in the throes of difficult conditions. Yet when the crisis is past, most allow renewed priority to be given to domestic customers, failing to see the real opportunities.

Set up long-term agreements

Arranging long-term contracts before the start of a downturn plainly provides a continuing source of revenue to carry you through the dry years. Sedco was able to look ahead.

> **Sedco.** This Dallas-based oil rig company with sales of $523 million in 1982 made conservative long-term agreements of up to five years in duration and brought its customers in as joint partners on its new rigs. By contrast, most competitors, with rental prices spiralling, had kept their agreements short to maximize their profits.
>
> When a massive industry downturn hit in 1982, 100 per cent of Sedco's 36 rigs were fully booked into the next year, whereas only 22 per cent of its competitors' rigs were employed at all. Sedco's chief executive officer, B Gill Clements, declared at the time: 'We may have missed the crest in rates, but at least we're not looking at an unemployed fleet.'

Lock in customers, lock out competitors

Market share is up for grabs as customers and suppliers rethink contracts. Then is the time for companies to challenge established competitors for new customers, and hence seize the revenue stream for the boom time to come.

A key to lucrative business can be the ability to lock in customers and lock out competitors. Maintaining high switching costs and providing significant customer benefits are essential in dissuading customers from talking to competitors.

In downturns, the emphasis of strategy turns to a competitor focus rather than a market focus: optimization of the product is sometimes not as important as blocking or limiting competitors' entry to that market. Factors which have never before been regarded as competitively important need to be exploited and the business restructured to match the company's strengths. An example of such forward thinking is that of Air Products.

> **Air Products.** In the 1970s this industrial gases manufacturer had the idea that instead of building large, centralized plants, which combined the benefit of economies of scale with the problem of long-distance distribution, it would link small, localized industrial oxygen plants to the manufacturing facilities of major customers. This had the added effect of locking in the customer and locking out the competition.

Reach more customers more cost effectively

It is the sheer expense of winning sales from new customers that has led me to emphasize the opportunity of generating revenue from existing customers. Ultimately, of course, this approach will reach its limits and developing new customers will be seen as critical to the enterprise. This section explores ways of making those efforts more cost effective. One of the most important factors in the success of any marketing campaign is knowing who the decision-maker is, what his needs are and, critically, how best he can be reached.

Who is the real decision-maker and what are his needs?

Companies are sometimes surprised to find that the nature of the decision-maker has changed. Those who can perceive such a change will have the edge on those who continue to target the now much less powerful, traditional customer contacts.

In hard times it is often the case that the customer's purse strings are held ever more tightly by the financial controllers instead of the users and technical specialists who used to make the buying decisions.

Not only does the identity of the decision-maker change, but his needs will be very different. His perception of what the company needs, and the style of dealing with him, must therefore reflect these factors.

Over time, customers tend to want different features from their purchases and suppliers. Often, it is only in difficult business conditions that this becomes apparent.

One possible factor in this trend is an increased degree of customer experience which can drive customers' greater price sensitivity. When a product is first introduced, for instance, customers are concerned about risk, and so support services and reliability become more important than price. However, over time, they build experience with the product, and as competitors move into the market the product appears undifferentiated. The purchase decision moves from applications to the procurement department. The result is that the customer becomes price sensitive. Companies who fail to recognize this, lose sales.

The supplier's response to the changes in customer needs, the identity of decision-makers, and their perceived needs must be to refocus his product's features and benefits on the new buyers and their perceived needs. Companies should reassess their techniques for reaching the true buyer and ensure that they reflect the new realities. You need to look hard at more cost-effective ways of presenting your product to these buyers, who have very different ways of doing business.

Better ways of reaching customers

It is the increased expense of a sales call compared to the cost and effectiveness of new techniques that is driving the emergence of new variants of old sales methods and a few novel approaches, while it has been changes in the cost of technology and lateral thinking that have made many new techniques a reality. The marketer's quiver has traditionally contained the alternatives of media ads, direct mail, telephone selling, trade shows, face-to-face selling and public relations. Many of these have benefited from new twists and have been augmented with national or key account management, demonstration centres, hotel presentations, telesales and new forms of catalogue selling. There are opportunities for those companies able to exploit fully these techniques in advance of the competition.

Key account management

National or key account management relies on the prudence of the Pareto

80/20 rule: of focusing on the areas most likely to have the biggest pay-offs.

Historically, key account management has concentrated on serving the needs of existing customers. When a customer comes to represent a significant amount of business, he will naturally tend to expect a greater level of service in return for his custom. In competitive times, when other suppliers are circling and making beguiling promises, the prudent company will be building up an understanding and strong relationship with the customer. While used mainly for existing customers, it can also be most gainfully employed in the search for additional customers.

When trying for new business, it makes sense to have a dedicated team for the customers with the greatest potential. That may be the only way to counter the attempts of existing suppliers to hold on to their customers. Then, when the opportunity comes, you will be better prepared to present your proposals than the competition because you have taken the time to come to understand his needs better and have set up an organization which is able to meet his needs best.

Demonstration centres

If your company sells products which are complex and not very portable, then you need to consider bringing the product and the customer together using a demonstration centre.

Many companies set aside space in their offices as demonstration areas for their products. Alternatively, trade associations often set up demonstration centres on their premises for the benefit of their members. Being permanent, they have the advantage of not having the fixed timing and transient nature of trade shows.

One of the best variants on the theme of a demonstration centre is a mobile truck: you take it to the customers. Of course, while you demonstrate your products, the customers are free of the 'distractions' of the competition. In addition, it can be particularly useful for reaching the higher-level executives who tend not to be available for selling presentations and may not go to the trade exhibitions, yet are maintaining greater control over their company's expenditure than before.

An example of what can be done with this idea is provided by a company in the packaging industry which, by using a carefully targeted direct mailing campaign, invited existing and potential customers to see the products in its demonstration truck at several convenient locations around the UK and Europe. For large, individual customers, the truck was positioned in their car parks and everyone at the site connected with the possible purchase could troop out to view the products. For the more dispersed smaller customers, hotel car parks near major motorway intersections proved to be excellent sites. The truck then went on to an exhibition where it stood outside the main entrance, raising the profile of the company and allowing the demonstration of specialized applications. The demonstration truck successfully recouped its investment from much increased product sales.

Hotel presentations

Here, the customer is brought to the sales person for a product presentation in a hotel room. The concept is particularly attractive where the value of a sale is too low to cover the travelling costs and the loss of selling time for an individual call. For products which need demonstration yet are relatively compact, easy to set up and are part of a narrow range, hotel presentations are ideal. IBM and Digital continue to use the idea to great success.

Telesales

Telesales has risen to prominence because it is so much cheaper than personal selling. A personal call may cost over £50 whereas a telephone call would probably cost less than £5. So instead of a sales person managing, say, five or six pitches per day, he can do 30 long telephone calls.

Telesales is a higher impact substitute for media and direct mail and so can replace slower, less convenient communications. While more expensive than direct mail, it has the advantage of allowing the operator to supply information, solicit feedback and answer customer objections. This makes telesales the most cost-effective method for small accounts where the margins on the product cannot justify personal calls. For existing customers, it can substitute for personal calls where the frequency of calls required outweighs the value of the product, and can help to nip any dissatisfaction in the bud.

Telesales can be a useful supplement to other marketing techniques in that freefone 1-800 (US) and 0800 (UK) numbers can help to convert a consumer buying impulse into an order, since it is easier to telephone than cut out a coupon and post it.

The state of the art in telephone selling is almost certainly defined by Allstate.

Allstate, the direct marketing wing of the Sears Group, owes much of its prominence to its highly effective use of telephone selling software. Holding information on some tens of millions of people in its database,

> Allstate can reach out and touch most of America by telephone.
>
> Just before making a sales call, the operator pulls up the details of the customer on the screen and then makes his pitch. As the customer raises objections, the operator can call up the relevant responses on his screen.
>
> This advanced software has substantially increased the sales person's success rate. Instead of spending just 25 minutes an hour actually selling, a phenomenal 43 minutes can now be devoted to a direct revenue-winning activity.

Direct mail

Direct mailing is a well-known method of accurately targeting potential customers who may be overcome by the morass of competing advertising. As an example of the possibilities, we turn again to Allstate.

> **Allstate** has access to the addresses and mail-order purchase history of 77 per cent of the 80 million US households from its links with the Sears empire. Using this information, Allstate is able to employ direct mail to target specific households with specific products. This has proved to be a highly effective marketing strategy. Industry observers estimate an astonishing return of investment on the effort of between 20 and 40 per cent, surely far in excess of most marketing techniques.

Catalogue selling

Many companies have had a great deal of marketing success from distributing a catalogue and providing a telephone number for the purpose of ordering products. They have recognized that the combination of catalogue and telephone has a greater impact than other forms of print, offers a real time saving for the customer, and provides closer coordination and control.

By tying up with a distributor selling to similar segments and for whom your product would be complementary, you might have your product included in his catalogues. Marketing costs are clearly reduced by this 'piggyback' approach.

Maintaining advertising

'Top management policy is that when others are cutting back in a critical area, we pour it on and get twice the bang for our buck', declared a director of a well-known financial services group in the US. Indeed, studies of over 100 companies undertaken on behalf of the American Business Press over a period of 20 years from 1956 [5] have consistently shown that spending on advertising in a recession can help to raise market share disproportionately. For instance, a sample of companies in a certain industrial sector was followed over a period of five years (1968–72), of which two were recession years. It was found that those who had maintained their advertising expenditure had benefited from a net income which had grown 50 per cent faster than those who had decreased their advertising budgets.

A similar study of public information of the US airline industry [6] found that those which had increased their advertising expenditure suffered negligible change in market share, compared to a 4 per cent decline for those who reduced their advertising expenditure for both recession years. Parallel research on the US auto market showed an increase of 3 per cent in market share for those which continued advertising against a 1 per cent decline for those which discontinued.

Not only can it be argued that the effectiveness of advertising is increased in difficult times, but it is also much cheaper. Advertising costs are considerably reduced in a recession as media buyers have been forced to negotiate and accept more than 20–30 per cent declines in rates. Some magazines have been known to offer free advertisements to fill space and to convince wavering clients to book space.

Some marketers raise the argument that consumer advertising is not worth much in a recession because nobody has any money. This can be countered by pointing out that the extra caution of the recession often causes families to put their income into savings accounts rather than in the cash registers. So, because families have the money but are curtailing their purchases, it is more, not less, coaxing by advertising that is required. During recessions and downturns, advertising should be anything but recessive.

Advertorial

'Advertorial', a hybrid of advertising and editorial, has proved to be a particularly effective way of getting publicity for many companies, big and small.

While this simple idea is well known in the US, it remains under exploited in the UK. Sending in information about your company on a regular basis and building a relationship with magazines and other media means you get mentioned as news. Such a relationship hardly comes for free of course; it will probably require a combination of placing some advertisements, lunches, tours of the company premises and previews of new products. That there is enormous potential in advertorial is shown by the experience of a client company. It is surprising that advertorial is not more commonly employed.

> **Packaging company.** Advertorial has long been a linchpin of this company's marketing strategy. The company typically places 15 adverts per year in trade magazines at a cost of £13,500. It also wins approximately 45 editorials over the same period of roughly a fifth of the size of the adverts, often with photographs. Notwithstanding the increased effectiveness of placing information in the editorial page, the space alone is equivalent to an additional 50 per cent of expenditure. The result has been that over a third of the company's total exposure each year continues to cost them next to nothing.

Word-of-mouth is free

Tom Peters, author of *In Search of Excellence*, points out the key strategic significance of word-of-mouth transfer of product information among potential customers – it's free. Not only that, word-of-mouth is probably the most cost-effective source of qualified leads that a company will ever get. Word-of-mouth comes from a person the customer sees as impartial, and therefore is highly influential. Word-of-mouth is an essential by-product of good service.

Perhaps you recall the results of a study which showed that satisfied customers told three other people of their good experiences, while unhappy customers told 11 other people of their woes. 'The best sales person is a satisfied customer' is an old saying which captures the essence of word-of-mouth. It should be carefully managed.

New products, new ideas

'Entrepreneurs with new concepts or products can thrive during economic downturn', wrote Victor Kiam, the chief executive officer of Remington consumer products. 'The old merchandise and ideas aren't selling, so retailers are willing to try anything that might stimulate trade.'

Sources of new product ideas

Of the many different methods for generating new product ideas, it has been found [7] that the most successful came from the following (in descending order of priority):

- Marketing think-tanks
- Market analysis
- Customer group discussions
- Customer in-depth interviews
- The R&D department
- Competitors' products

- Overseas sister company
- The company's advertising agency
- Analysis of market segmentation
- Suppliers.

When devising new products for the consumer market, many companies have come to grief by relying on the opinions of their trade customers. However, it is surprising how often distributors can be so badly out of tune with their customers. A clock manufacturer, for instance, had developed a new product range which was enthusiastically received by the trade. On launch, however, it was totally rejected by the very female consumers who made up the majority of the market, and at whom the product was specifically aimed.

I shall concentrate on just a few specific opportunities here. Some of the most powerful and effective ideas are those which come from abroad, and from rethinking the customer's value chain in order to come up with a substitution product. These sources are now examined.

Ideas from abroad

Scouting abroad for new product ideas is not a new idea but it is surprisingly underexploited. Just how significant it is, is highlighted by the classic example of the potato.

> **The potato**. Most of us rely on the potato for our source of daily carbohydrates. Yet its introduction as an essential part of our diet is attributed to the Elizabethan adventurer Sir Walter Raleigh of more than four centuries ago. Having been discovered on a foray into the South American subcontinent, the humble potato has since been re-exported to the Americas, becoming an essential constituent in the success of Ray Kroc, the progenitor of McDonald's, the world's leading burger and fries restaurant chain.

Most big companies nowadays make a point of systematically scanning the world for new product ideas. The advent of cheaper information flow means that this avenue is now open to smaller companies too.

Unlike brand names and technology, product ideas have little legal protection and are therefore open to export. Since a large proportion of new products fail in the marketplace, borrowing a proven idea from overseas can significantly reduce costs. In the case of consumer products, in particular, this process can avoid the significant risk of boring customers.

The feeling of Elizabeth Harrington, corporate director of consumer product marketing at US consultants A T Kearney Inc, was that 'instead of spending all this money on R&D, let's go to the treasure trove in Europe and Asia'.

Imported product ideas which are thought to have the greatest potential are those which are widely distributed abroad by the biggest companies. The dry beers, for example, which became best sellers for the US brewing giants were allegedly originally pioneered by Sapporo Breweries and Asahi Breweries in Japan.

Products from abroad have to be better than the existing domestic product and they need to be compatible with customer habits back home, as Kellogg recognized when it brought its breakfast cereal 'Mueslix' to the US after studying the mixtures of fruit, nuts and cereals to be found in Europe.

Foreign subsidiaries can be extremely useful as listening posts. Indeed, some companies set up small foreign operations specifically for this purpose.

It is well known that certain countries are in the vanguard of certain developments. For example, the US is several years ahead of the UK in the use of computers in direct mail. An enterprising company would therefore ensure its executives regularly visited the US to look for good business ideas that it could transplant at home. Clarke Hooper is just such a company.

Clarke Hooper is the UK's only sales promotion agency quoted on the Stock Exchange. Active in persuading people to buy products through the use of competitions and discounts, Clarke Hooper often transfers good ideas from the US half of the company to the UK.

One US development that they are reported to have been studying, for example, is a technique for electronic sales promotion at a supermarket counter where the customer is bombarded with a sales message specific to his purchase. The company 'is convinced these techniques will soon be commonplace in the UK' and is well placed to take advantage of the opportunity to introduce such ideas.

Continuing with the theme of food retailing, the success of Sainsbury's, market leader in the UK, has often been attributed to it being the first to bring the supermarket concept to Britain after a director made an exploratory trip to the US.

A trawl for good ideas in foreign markets can be a very effective way of coming up with the winning product the customers are looking for.

Developing new products

R&D is rarely a flow of water which can be turned on like a tap when a new product is required. In most fields of business, the long lead time of new product development is such that companies who choose to cut back on R&D in difficult economic conditions are often at a disadvantage to those who take the opportunity to maintain their spending.

However, it may not always be such a drawn out affair. Product redesign and customization can offer the scope of rapid innovation. For instance, a manufacturer of small consumer durables was able to effect the appearance of a complete remodelling exercise for over 60 per cent of its range without having to retool by the creative use of cosmetic design changes using the old tooling.

Many R&D programmes take longer than they need to. ICI Fibres discovered this when it came under severe pressure in 1984 from a competitor threat and a marketplace which was clamouring for new products. By really focusing on customer needs and instilling a highly motivated attitude among the teams, the whole research, development and engineering process for the new product, reported the technical director, was telescoped into three or four years, when normally this would have taken six or seven years.

Customize

Customization of products and services has been used successfully in the past to lock in a customer to a relationship which then survives through difficult economic times to the boom times. The technique shuts out competitors by fulfilling customer needs better.

Customized semiconductor chips are a good example. 'Despite the recession in the semiconductor industry', stated an analyst during an industry recession in 1984, 'the customized market is expected to grow 10 to 20 per cent, considerably faster than the market for standard circuits.'

Substitution

Adopting the customer's viewpoint

'People buy 1/4-inch drill bits', wrote Ted Levitt, marketing guru at Harvard Business School, 'but need 1/4-inch holes.' Products are bought for the service they provide to the customer. Looking differently at the value provided by a product and the real need of the customer often requires considerable lateral thinking.

It is the replacing of a product by a substitute with improved value for the customer which provides the real opportunity of new product innovation in a downturn. Substitution products offer so much opportunity in that they allow companies to circumvent entry barriers erected by former market leaders and typically re-establish new ones in their place. There is no better time to introduce such new ideas.

The soft drinks packaging market, which has been particularly beset by substitution over the 1980s, serves to demonstrate the rapid changes possible. The drive to provide improved value for the customer and a profit opportunity for the supplier has produced cheaper, lighter, more convenient soft drinks packaging. Only a decade or so ago, for instance, all soft drinks were supplied in glass bottles. Then aluminium cans were introduced, which led to retaliation from the ferrous metal companies in the form of thin tin plate. Now, plastic and waxed paper are very common. The change to a different material and distribution chain provided significant competitive opportunities for alert companies.

One of the most outstandingly successful forms of substitution is represented by Nucor. It replaced one traditional process with another so that it could offer its customers better value and prosper against bigger competitors.

Nucor has consistently run the most productive steel mills in the USA. Nucor represents a new type of mill: the 'minimill'. A modified production process at its Compact Strip Production facility at Crawfordsville, Indiana allows Nucor to use scrap steel as its raw material. It therefore does not need the extremely expensive ovens required by its competitors, the integrated mills, to process steel from the raw ore. By substituting a lower energy process, with its resultant lower construction costs, Nucor has managed to circumvent one of the high entry barriers enjoyed by the biggest player, US Steel (now USX).

The results from rethinking the entire process have been astonishing. In 1980, a desperate time for steel, Nucor was achieving an exceptional return on equity – almost 30 per cent. With the ability to build plants for under a tenth of the cost of the integrated mills, and with productivity 20 per cent better than Japan, and more than 40 per cent better than the US companies, Nucor has been able to sell steel more cheaply than imports. In addition, the nature of the process allows the company to make small runs of products, which meets customer needs better. It is no wonder that US Steel chose to exit the markets where it could not compete with Nucor. Nucor owes its success to the ability of its founders to envisage a substitute process.

People Express. When no-frills airline People Express (PE) was launched, it planned to compete on cost with other airlines as well as other forms of transport. Its service was therefore designed to substitute for bus, train or car.

The advantage of travelling with PE was self-evident when considering the company's original figures for the cost of a journey from Newark, New Jersey to Palm Beach, Florida. A car at that time was estimated to cost $250 at 20 cents per mile for the trip; a bus or train would cost $130; and PE would cost under $89. PE therefore attempted to substitute for cars, buses and trains on long routes with a great deal of ground traffic.

Competitive Opportunity

The impact of microelectronics in the late 1970s provided many opportunities for companies able to mobilize behind the new technology. One such company is the GEC Avery weighing machine company which, in the space of three short years at the turn of the 1980s, managed to convert almost all of its electromechanical products to electronics. As a result, the proportion sold with electronics moved from 30 to 90 per cent. GEC Avery continues to dominate its market.

Services and products can be equivalent

Services can substitute for products and vice versa. Products and services can therefore be equivalent to the customer in providing him with a solution to his needs. For example, many do-it-yourself products make it possible to do activities which previously had to be done by a skilled craftsman hired for the job.

The concept of solving a customer's needs more cost effectively is a rich vein of opportunities waiting to be tapped.

Chapter 9

Avoiding the Slide into Price Cuts

Significant bottom line impact

Pricing, one of the most important factors in business, is also one of the least understood. It may even be the most difficult single decision that a firm has to make. In the chemical industry of 1991, for example, an independent consultant estimated that, for the average European company, a 1 per cent fall in prices would cut profits as much as a 5 per cent decline in volume. As for the customer, price is usually the prime area for negotiation when making a purchase. Therefore, pricing warrants considerable study.

Pricing intelligently helps in leaving less money on the table when in competition with another supplier, in shaving prices to gain volume without provoking competitive retaliation, and in being able to quote a higher price without risking the loss of an order or a long-term relationship.

In difficult times, competitive pressures are greater, and so it is much more difficult to make immediate gains in market share. In static markets therefore the emphasis shifts inevitably to margins. It is because prices are often the quickest way to impact margins that two chapters have been devoted to the opportunities provided by the price dimension. This chapter deals with raising prices and avoiding the need to reduce price: the very impact of reduced prices being so great, it is important to put effort into preventing price cuts. However, this process is not always achievable in really severe conditions. For this reason, the next chapter explains ways of making the most of price reductions, and how a low price can be handled as an important competitive weapon.

This chapter is divided into three sections:

- 'The whole product' deals with differentiating the product from its competitors by ensuring that all the product's features are brought into view.
- 'Perception is reality' is concerned with the customer perceiving that the product represents better value to him.
- 'Raise prices' combines the previous ideas to increase margins opportunistically.

Product augmentation, another strategy for delaying competition on price, has been covered in Chapter 8.

Anybody can sell on price

This is probably a sales manager's most commonly voiced comment in difficult times. It is, after all, generally easy to move goods or churn customers by reducing prices (except in the extreme case where the customer won't take the product even if you pay him). But unless you are the lowest cost producer in the industry, the skill lies in maintaining profits by holding up margins – and that means prices.

Prices drop because it is the easiest short-term measure to win sales and because buyers are themselves under pressure to demand more for less. 'No one', as the expression goes, 'has ever met the person who first cut the price.' It only takes one supplier to be desperate to find a buyer to cause price pressure throughout a market and all players will be tempted to cut their prices in response.

But it is because the product's advantages have not been fully developed that price appears to be the only competitive weapon available. The prevalence of price-cutting in many markets indicates that a great deal of opportunity lies here. All the product's features and benefits have to be brought into play. That is the theme of the 'whole product'.

The whole product

The total package

The 'product' is the total package of benefits the customer receives when he buys. Customers' clamouring for lower prices should not hide the fact that the price is only one part of the value of the product. Therefore, to avoid the customer thinking just in terms of price, the manager must emphasize the many dimensions of value represented by the product.

'All things are relative': it is the difference between all of the benefits of the product and that of the competition which determines who gets the sale, and whether high margins can be demanded. That means being different in a way that's important to the customer. Thus, prices should be based on a product-by-product comparison with competitors' prices, competitive advantages and disadvantages, and desired position in the marketplace.

A particularly useful method for presenting the information in a meaningful way is the use of a 2 × 2 matrix (see overleaf). For each distinct market sector, a square box is drawn with the customers' purchase criteria ranked on a scale of 0 –100 per cent on one axis, and the customers' ratings of the competing products (including substitutes) on the other axis. The box is then divided into four, as shown in the diagram. The top right-hand square is the area where most attention should be placed. Using this approach you can readily see where you can raise prices when a product feature is unique and highly prized, and at what level to set prices to overcome any perceived product disadvantage. The matrix is also useful in finding gaps in the market for new products and services.

Products which may act as substitutes should also be brought into the equation. For example, a pizza parlour will compete with a burger bar for a consumer's money.

All goods and services are differentiable

It was Ted Levitt, Harvard Business School professor, who showed that 'there is no such thing as a commodity. All goods and services are differentiable'. So avoiding the slide into price cuts means differentiating the product in the customers' eyes. The life assurance example shows how critical this can be.

Life assurance. A life assurance company in Edinburgh, Scotland offered a certain policy at similar rates to all the other companies. There were, it should be granted, minor differences between the policies but the customer would have to do a lot of digging to find which was the very best deal. In essence, the companies and their products were not perceived as being differentiated.

At the life assurance company in question, managers were looking for some way of differentiating themselves from the competition. They decided they would respond more quickly to letters received. By watching the age of correspondence in the 'in-tray', the company was able to build up a reputation for efficiency and speed which gave it a key competitive edge.

Where differentiation of products by their features is difficult, then the emphasis must turn towards more intangible aspects of the product, such as service, quality, risk, convenience and delivery options. These are all part of the 'whole product'. Several examples of intangibles are now highlighted.

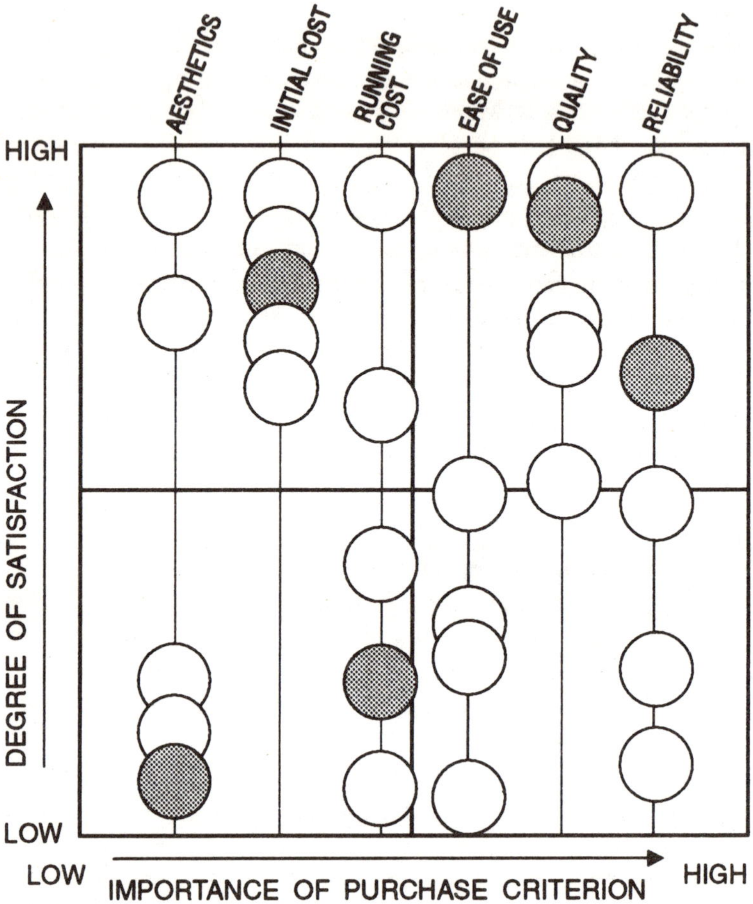

How customers rate competing products

Customer support and reduced risk perception

Many companies have found that providing back-up, either initially or on an ongoing basis, is a keystone in maintaining high margins. Support is also important for new players and unsophisticates who are willing to pay for peace of mind. Naturally, companies have to be careful to provide an appropriate level of service: providing unwanted or low-value services does not materially improve competitive advantage.

IBM is a classic example of being able to generate higher-than-average margins in this way. 'IBM', as the saying goes, 'doesn't have better product. It has better sales persons.' IBM's competitive advantage, which has endured over so many years, particularly in mainframe computers, is based on the support it provides in ensuring an integrated total solution to customers' problems.

Where vast amounts of money are required to be spent on a product, and a great deal of downside risk is involved, then buyers, whose careers may well be jeopardized by a bad decision, tend to play safe. IBM is again the illustration: 'Nobody ever gets fired for buying IBM.' IBM has built up a reputation for not letting its customers down, and so buying from such a brand name is considered a safe bet.

Charging more for faster delivery

Better delivery performance can be a useful differentiator. Can you perhaps be more flexible in helping the customer to avoid the inevitable snags? Reordering responsiveness is even more important in hard times. Being able to help with customers' shortages can win loyalty which can be translated into higher margins.

Charging for convenience

While customers in difficult business climates often try to save money by bringing many activities in-house, they still value anything which makes life easier for them, as long as the cost is not too excessive. Being able to provide a 'one-stop shop', where they can quickly find many of their requirements, is a useful way of building up competitive advantage and differentiating from the competition. Another avenue is providing an extended range of products and services by selling someone else's service at a profit.

Perception is reality

Beauty is in the eye of the beholder

'A customer attaches value to a product in proportion to its perceived ability to help solve his problems or meet his needs', writes Ted Levitt. For the customer making a purchase decision, the value of the product is therefore the value he perceives it to be.

Buyers have different buying behaviour and different needs. Some, for example, place greater emphasis on essentials and short-term price goals, whereas others are less sensitive to price and are looking for an enhanced product. Companies therefore need to show how the product meets each buyer's specific needs.

Where a customer has a choice of alternative suppliers and feels he has nothing to choose between them, then the product is seen by the customer as a commodity. One definition of a commodity is a product whose producer has no real control over the price. Hence, it is vital to prevent the product being seen as a commodity, if pressure on price is to be averted.

When there is excess capacity in a commodity industry, for example, with all the players desperate to sell, then the situation often becomes very painful. To avoid such machinations, many companies move to specialized markets where high value can be added. For instance, ICI, the UK chemical manufacturer, spent a decade moving away from commodity and bulk products. The recession of the early 1990s indicated that its speciality business units had held up well, but the bulk products which remained were badly affected by the downturn and had, in the words of an industry observer, 'gone off the cliff in just the same way as before'.

Account management

We have already considered the increasing move in some companies towards centralizing buying decisions and putting the responsibility in the hands of the financial management. This provides an opportunity, which is well exploited by IBM, which staffs its account management teams with a higher level of reps to ensure high-level representation on the customer's side. Thus, by talking to more senior financially orientated personnel, IBM is able to take the issues away from direct price comparison by the purchasing department, and from detailed technical appraisal by the technical people. In this way, it is able to stress the competitive advantages of the 'whole product' it offers its customers.

Funny money

Since the customer buys on his perceptions of the value of the product, companies should look carefully at expressing the product benefits in such a way as to further improve the customer's perception. This is the concept of 'funny money'.

Funny money works by dividing up the total amount, representing an outlay of cash whose sheer size would frighten the customer, into smaller more manageable chunks. The well-known British sales trainer, John

Winkler, recalls the story of his wanting to find somewhere to moor his 8-metre catamaran. On asking how much it would cost to leave his boat in the marina, the owner of the site explained that, faced with a similar task, he had paid for it by giving up smoking a couple of packets of cigarettes a day. In this way, he had made the sum seem trivial and therefore managed to reduce the customer's perception of the cost.

Cost of ownership

Cost of ownership calculations, a variant on funny money, is a surprisingly underused concept for selling durable products.

When a product costs several thousand pounds, the customer's perception of the cost is changed when a sales person explains that, over the life of the product, the costs represent only a few hundred pounds per year, or so many pounds per wash (for a washing machine).

Cost of ownership can be a useful way of minimizing the perceived difference in price of a product whose initial cost appears high compared to the competition. By adding in all costs over the lifetime of the product, including service and consumables, a comparison of costs per week or per unit output will narrow considerably. The premium which remains can then be justified by highlighting the features of the product which provide significant advantages. For example, an industrial capital equipment manufacturer performed a cost of ownership comparison between its own and the competitors' products. It found it was charging £10 more per week and looked for a way to justify this premium to its more price-sensitive customers. Recognizing that its customers valued reliability more than anything else, the company referred to the added cost of its reliability-improving features as an 'insurance policy' of £10 per week. For customers, this represented a trivial amount compared to the cost of their production line being shut down by the manufacturer's product breaking down.

Another way of reducing the perceived cost of a product is to point out its likely resale value and the low risk of getting that value. Offering part-exchange deals is one possibility. IBM, for example, was initially compelled to set up a secondary market for some of its mainframes by encouraging middlemen to buy second-hand computers and sell them on.

Higher margins on smaller cost items

Increasing prices and passing on inflationary cost increases is easier on smaller items because even a large percentage increase in the cost of a low-value item will have hardly any noticeable effect on the customer's final costs. Manufacturers of nuts, bolts and screws are notorious opportunists in this fashion.

A variant on this concept is that which minimizes the customer's cash flow problems by reconfiguring the product in smaller packets. So instead of having to buy in large quantities, they can buy just when they need it.

Higher margins are not only possible on smaller cost items, but also on products which represent a small proportion of a customer's costs. Managers tend to focus their attention on those few purchases that represent a significant proportion of costs. As a result, suppliers frequently generate their highest margins on purchases that represent a small proportion of the buyer's total costs.

Leasing and pay-as-you-use

Hire purchase or leasing minimizes the customer's initial outlay and helps to reduce his perception of the product's cost. This option, of letting the customer have the benefit of the product before he has the cash, has been the cause of many a growth market.

By reducing the perception of the cost of a product and minimizing the up-front investment by the customer, a 'pay-as-you-use' strategy has been the basis for many companies' success. Xerox is a well-known example. It owes its market dominance of the photocopier market not only to its recognition of the potential of the new-fangled device, but also to its innovative pricing strategy. By installing a counter on each machine, it was able to charge the customer only a certain number of cents per copy, with no additional charges. Customers no longer had to concern themselves with whether they could ensure a guaranteed volume of work for the machine, and were willing to pay a premium.

Higher prices for irregularly purchased items

Comprehensive studies of consumer behaviour of housewives buying their groceries have been extended to show that customers are less sensitive to price rises on irregularly purchased items. Since they are unable to remember exactly what the price was last time, they appear to be able to reconcile themselves with the new price by ascribing it to costs related to time (such as inflation). Hence, there is more flexibility to raise prices with irregularly purchased products. Naturally, the situation may well be different if a central purchasing department with easily accessible records is involved with an industrial product.

Raise prices

Going for the highest possible price

How many companies actually price on what the market will stand? By not doing so, many opportunities are being missed in every industry sector.

Raising prices can provide one of the fastest ways of increasing cash flow, so long as the loss of volume is offset by the rise in profit per unit.

Many managers are over-cautious in increasing prices, but raising prices need not be as risky as it sounds. Price rises can be cancelled, or selectively withdrawn by offering discounts to key customers, which makes it easier to raise prices to the list price level once demand strengthens.

Analyzing the record of the company's 'won and lost' quotes for a particular customer is important in establishing the company's current price position with the customer. An understanding of the most recent prices paid by the customer will serve to determine the customer's price threshold.

Managers also need to identify those customers who are the most vendor loyal (those who buy regularly regardless of price fluctuations) and those who are unable to go elsewhere (because of high switching costs, or the lack of credible competitors).

Setting the price will also be critically influenced by current competitor price levels, taking into account likely discounts and non-price concessions.

A good example of managing the process effectively is as follows.

> **Marketing manager's database.** A marketing manager collected information about all his major customers. This included the latest quotes by competitors to several customers and ranked customers on price sensitivity, visibility to competition, and strength of supplier relationship. In this way, after a year or so, he was able to predict the customer's behaviour and so design the pricing strategy for each customer. The pay-off came when he was able to raise average prices 15 per cent without announcing a general price increase and managed to raise his volume by 10 per cent.

Customer research, particularly talking to the more important customers, is critical. Performing the research at a distance has its uses of course, but with the proviso that the sales-force earn their commission on volume, not on profits. So asking them about raising prices is not likely to produce a positive response unless their earnings are linked to profits.

Sharp increases

For those customers who are least price sensitive, making sharp increases in price-insensitive items can achieve a greater overall average price than through an across-the-board adjustment. In one extreme case, a company supplying a unique industrial controller, finding that it had a unique position in an important product item, was able to increase the price of that item four-fold, and with negligible loss of customers. As a result, it improved its overall corporate profits by 25 per cent.

Managing competitors

One of the reasons why managing companies is so difficult, especially in downturns, is that competitors can respond to your moves. Managing prices therefore requires an element of managing your competitors in allowing for their reactions, as BTR's Rockware shows.

> **Rockware Glass.** When Frank Davies took over as chief executive of Rockware Glass in the UK in the middle of a price war, he quickly increased prices by 7.5 per cent. Rockware lost volume but, within a month, the expected closure of several competitor plants and a strike at dominant player United Glass had brought much of the business back. Two months later the competitors followed the lead. Less than a year afterwards, Rockware again upped prices – this time by 8 per cent as the customers renegotiated their prices – and competitors followed suit.

If competitors decide to raise prices, you have to decide whether to follow them upwards by the same amount, or even at all. If you do not increase prices by the same amount, you have to consider whether the increase in your unit volume caused by your relatively lower price is sufficient to compensate for the increased margins that could be achieved by following competitors upwards.

The effect on volume from increasing or decreasing prices relative to the competition can be estimated and a judgement made as to what course of action to take. A manager wishing to increase prices should ask the sales-force for its opinions on what reduction in sales demand the company should expect for a given percentage increase in price. It is then a simple matter to calculate the critical loss of volume after which less profit would be produced. If the volume loss expected by the sales-force is less than the critical volume loss calculated, then it would be profitable to raise prices. For example, if the product's price at present is $100 per unit and the variable costs are $75 per unit, then the percentage contribution is 25 per cent. For a 15 per cent price rise, the critical volume loss can be shown to be 37.5 per cent; that is, the company's situation would be improved so long as volume does not fall more than 37.5 per cent. If sales and marketing had estimated a fall in volume of some 15–30 per cent, then this would flash a green light to the price rise. Inevitably, such estimates are best used only as a guide – they are clearly sensitive to the sales-force estimate of drop in sales volume. More detailed market research, especially among the bigger customers, should be considered to hone the idea.

One word of warning about raising prices. Firms which increase prices early to recover overheads as the demand falls often have an unfortunate tendency to maintain their raised prices despite their becoming desperately uncompetitive as the economy recovers. Then, when the top management finally come to realize that the continued volume falls are due to loss of price competitiveness, suicidally large and indiscriminate discounts are scattered far and wide with the aim of buying back market share. Clearly, managers should respond carefully to the market situation.

Stop losing money on your products through inflation

We have considered the factors of customers and competitors on raising price. But it is truly amazing the number of companies who are so unaware of their costs that they are actually selling products at a loss. Now is the time for a proper review. Managers should look hard at instantly raising prices on loss-making products, or axing them.

Inflation can severely reduce the profit of any operation if prices cannot be raised at the same rate. Inflation adjustments will naturally have a bigger effect on low-margin businesses, and the companies in danger are those who are not aware of the creeping growth of their costs until far too late.

As customers are aware of the progress of inflation, inflation is often a good reason for justifying price rises.

Where applicable, escalation and progress payment schedules should be built into contracts in times of high inflation. Pricing to pre-empt cost increases can become essential in earning an acceptable profit. Replacement cost projections are more useful here than those based on historical records. Some projects that look fine on an historical cost basis may actually be losers in real terms. Speeding up the pricing adjustment mechanism would allow a faster response.

Charge for everything

Many companies continue to provide extraneous services which add little value to the customer yet can cost the supplier a great deal. They may be unaware that customers only continue to accept such services because the full cost does not appear to be passed on to them, and not because they really want the services.

In these situations, where additional products and services are truly not adding much competitive advantage, or where the customers are locked in, you should look hard at charging for everything. This will have the dual effect of reducing unnecessary costs by not serving those customers who do not value the extra product, and of gaining profits from those who do. Companies who fail to ensure that customers pay only for those services they want can expect to be undercut by competitors. The whole process of avoiding the slide into price cuts can depend on charging for everything.

Are you charging for delivery and special services, invoicing the customer for non-warranty repairs on purchased equipment, and billing him for supervision of installation? Companies should make customers pay for the overtime required to meet rush orders, and for the interest on their overdue accounts. Can the minimum order size be increased? Can you cream off a higher margin by using different mark-ups on different sizes (particularly for consumer products)? Are you charging extra for special orders? It is important to look hard at ways of charging for everything and not leave unnecessary money on the table.

Unbundling

The process of charging for everything should be extended across the whole product range. This is the time to split the product range, providing the original 'bundled' package with all elements included, and a basic 'unbundled' offering. Focusing on the core product, cutting back to the bare bones and charging for all extras is the strategy.

The process is like the maturing of a market, where the priorities also change. For example, as industrial goods customers gain experience with the products they are buying, their needs change. At first, as inexperienced generalists, they want broad-based, packaged, highly serviced and supported products. Later, as experienced specialists, they want low-priced, unbundled, fixed-specification reliability.

Start low and add extra margin

Part of charging for everything and reducing the customer's initial perception is to take a basic price and add extra features to increase the margin. Consider the case of motor cars, for example. The initial price which attracts you into the showroom is that of the basic model. It is only then that the sales person sells you all about those high-margin extras you 'could not possibly do without'.

Chapter 10

Dropping Prices

There may eventually come a time when prices cannot be held up any longer. It is at times like these that, as in 1991, companies like Ford announce a 10 per cent cut in list prices, when a customer can win a 25 per cent discount on cars from dealers with little effort, and when companies such as Toshiba, Hewlett-Packard and IBM announce falls in price of between 33 and 60 per cent on their computers.

This chapter is about not leaving money on the table, dropping prices where you have to and holding prices where possible. It deals with disguising price drops, the advantages of dropping openly, the importance of variable pricing and selective discounts, and the three types of pricing. The opportunity of exploiting a low cost base to allow low prices to be used as a competitive weapon is discussed in some detail.

Disguising price falls

Many companies are wont to drop prices immediately to stimulate demand. They do this without thought for the future, when customers will not be so sensitive about price. Companies should therefore be circumspect in broadcasting their reductions.

Low visibility price reductions

It is well known that customers perceive a higher-priced product to possess superior quality to a lower-priced article. Hence, the notion that price is shorthand for quality should lead marketers of higher-quality products to be careful about lowering prices to stimulate demand. When some form of reduction is necessary, it becomes important to control the image of quality, the pricing structure after the downturn and, most importantly, what happens in other markets. All difficult economic conditions come to an end eventually and managers should consider the longer-term effects of their immediate decisions on quality perceptions and future prices.

Offering additional benefits and altering the terms of trade are quite common ways of winning the sale and maintaining control over price when dealing with the next customer. Other ideas for keeping low visibility on reduced prices are reduced service charges and even product changes. The business jet manufacturer, Gulfstream Aerospace, employed lateral thinking in offering 12 months' free fuel to customers who ordered new Commander executive jets. This produced orders for 20 planes: a significant quantity. In contrast, Chrysler discovered the limits of the approach when in the past it used a wide variety of deals to clear inventory: rebates, roll-backs of prices and zero or low interest rates on purchases. Unfortunately, consumers sometimes came to believe that the special deals were a routine part of car purchasing, so when business turned up and these practices were dropped, this attitude was shown to affect business badly for a considerable time.

Bartering, where companies sell in moneyless transactions, can be a successful tactic in a downturn since it disguises large discounts without destroying the price structure. Originally used in trade with firms in countries possessing non-exchangeable currency, the process has since been extended to wider business applications.

A particularly creative example of a hidden price drop is that of Hardy Spicer, manufacturer of constant velocity joints for automobiles. Short of demand, the company offered many of its customers long-term contracts which, because of their price control clauses, in effect promised to reduce prices to the customers in real (inflation-adjusted) terms.

Dropping prices openly

Reducing price and advertising the move is a traditional method designed to stimulate sales rapidly. Its success depends on the level of the cost base of the company and critically, how sensitive (or 'elastic') customer demand is to price.

Price sensitivity

Understanding how important customers rate price is critical when deciding on the level of price drops. As different customers will have different values, the market should be subdivided to take this into account.

The sensitivity of a segment's demand to price is often difficult to evaluate and so can require significant field experience. The economist's 'price elasticity' concept, which in its most simplistic form attempts to show that demand is linked only to price, is generally useful only as a thinking guide; it is often unworkable as a predictive tool. It is hard to apply, for example, where competitive products are highly differentiated and depend on non-financial factors such as service, styling, packaging, promotions, and back-up of spare parts. In addition, organizations cannot easily hold constant the important influences on sales demand that an economist assumes constant for analytical purposes (for example, advertising). Price elasticity concepts also have limited application where any buyer or seller is big enough to influence demand.

For these reasons, few companies will know precisely the shape of their demand curve (that is, what the demand will be at what price). However, using judgements borne of experience, an approximate relationship can be drawn. This can then be employed to examine contributions to indicate whether dropping prices to increase volume can increase the return to the company.

Some companies have found that some sectors' price sensitivity has in the past been so badly misjudged that profits can actually be decreased by dropping prices.

The facade of good value

An unusual variant on dropping prices openly is the clever behaviour of several American airlines.

> **US airlines.** Faced with severe competition after deregulation of the US air routes in the early 1980s, many airline companies recognized that low price had become a key purchase criterion. So passengers were exhorted to fly with each company by announcements of their special low fares. Yet behind the scenes the big carriers were adding conditions and limiting the applicability of their discount fares. In this way the airline companies were in fact reducing the number of their discount seats, all the while maintaining the facade of cheap fares.

When cutting prices doesn't help sales

Price cuts may not actually increase demand one jot if all competitors follow suit. Cutting prices may then prove to be a no-win situation, as is shown in the unhappy saga of the European steel industry.

> **European steel industry.** In the European steel industry recessions of 1974–5 and 1980–1, the average company needed 80 per cent capacity utilization to achieve break-even. Unfortunately, supply exceeded demand and 55 per cent was the average utilization. The typical reaction in this position is to drop price to bring demand in line with supply. So all companies dropped their prices, only to find that nobody bought any more steel – and everyone was worse off.

It is interesting to compare the approaches of the airlines and the steel makers. Lowering air fares (or giving that impression) is very likely to increase demand – either by simply stimulating price-sensitive demand or by taking business away from substitutes (trains, etc). But lowering steel prices is unlikely to switch customers from a substitute such as a plastic since the materials cannot be easily substituted for each other.

Variable pricing

Having got to the stage of having to give open discounts, managers now have to be selective in awarding them. In addition, they must avoid their motives being interpreted as anti-competitive. Offering variable discounts to exclude a competitor, for example, can be found predatory in both the US and Europe. These important factors will now be examined in more detail.

Selective discounts

'If we did all our deals like that we would be out of business.' Managers have to be very selective in allowing discounts, especially when the price does not cover all the overheads attributed to an order.

Suitable precautions are to dump your product well away from your usual market, using selective discounts to clear excess stocks as a one-off move. Repeat business should be conducted wherever possible at normal prices. Companies should be careful that the low price level does not set a precedent with their big customers, or that news of the low price spreads through the market so that other customers will come demanding the same treatment.

Different price levels for different customer groups require strong controls to prevent the sales-force, faced with manipulative customers and their monthly volume targets, allowing themselves to be pressured into giving indiscriminate discounts. This would have the effect of dragging general prices down to the lowest customer level.

Understand the legislation

Most countries have laws which regulate industry to try to prevent anti-competitive practices – to ensure that the playing field remains level. Not only is it important that companies do not overstep the relevant legislation, but they should not appear to do so. Taking advantage of the competitive opportunity of pricing therefore requires knowledge of the rules.

In the US the Robinson-Patman, Sherman and Clayton Acts cover variable pricing. In Europe it is the Treaty of Rome which applies, ruling against 'applying dissimilar conditions to equivalent transactions with other trading parties, thereby placing them at a competitive disadvantage'.

However, industry regulators are cognizant of the fact that the pressure of competition in a particular market is likely to cause a range of prices. Thus, the fact that price differentials exist across markets may merely indicate differing levels of competition and not necessarily predatory activity.

There is one case in which openly reducing price may actually be shown to be in the interests of customers. Persuading customers to change to a product they are not familiar with (either by direct replacement, or a new product) may require a drop in price to overcome the switching costs of perceived risk of not meeting specifications on performance and delivery.

The boundaries of legislation are further defined later in this chapter in 'Using a low cost base as a competitive weapon', page 144.

Price differentials based on cost

Defence against the legislation protecting companies from anti-competitive pricing usually demands that a reduction in price to one customer be justified by the lower cost of providing the product to that customer. Arguments for price differentials therefore have to be based on being able to show that customers can be segregated into classes and that the cost of serving each varies. Ideas include differentials based on size of order, method of delivery, timing of sales, speed of collection, distance, cooperative advertising allowances, provision of selling and technical services, warehousing, storage credit, sales management, manufacturing cost, installation, repair and maintenance, return, and trade-in allowances and rebates. Areas to avoid are resale price maintenance, below-cost reductions, price leadership, price signalling, price discrimination and new market entry pricing, all of which can present legal pitfalls.

An example of cost differentiation arguments in action is that of IBM.

> **IBM** has in the past offered a volume procurement discount: a discount for a customer agreeing to buy a set number of units by a given time. One example is a deal on buying 60 medium-sized computers within a period of 18 months. These so-called 'special bids' were designed to link prices to IBM's cost of making the sale. John Opel, the then-chairman of IBM, said: 'When they buy an automobile, some people go in and take test drives and take up the time of 15 different salesmen. Others read a magazine, then go to a showroom and say "I want this". There are different costs associated with these transactions, and to be competitive you have to acknowledge them.'

Negotiating prices

Since most industrial prices are negotiated, price differentiation among customer groups is frequently an important key to profit.

Industrial products tend to be custom made or modified, and therefore have different costs. Hence, the various regulations prove comparatively less burdensome than for consumer goods because of a greater latitude in setting prices. In addition, because most industrial customers do not compete head on, it can be argued that they need not be charged the same price by a given supplier.

The three types of pricing

Beyond selective discounting, there are three important groups of pricing strategies that companies should be aware of. These are marginal pricing, predatory pricing and low cost-base pricing

To an observer outside a company, such as a competitor, low cost-base and marginal pricing may be mistaken for predatory pricing. The latter, because it is commonly seen as an attempt to oust competitors by pricing well below costs, typically excites a frenzied competitor reaction, and can be illegal. This, it goes without saying, is something to be avoided. It is therefore important to understand and communicate the differences between these modes of operation.

Low cost-base pricing requires having the lowest cost base in the industry and lowering prices to such an extent that your company is still making a profit when others cannot. Exploiting this opportunity is covered later in the chapter.

Marginal pricing, often used to fill capacity, refers to price reductions which cover the direct costs but with less than the full standard allocation of overhead.

Marginal pricing

Marginal pricing presents the opportunity to win an order that would otherwise be lost and thereby make a positive contribution to the fixed costs of the company. Pricing above average variable costs and below average total costs, marginal pricing is presumed lawful.

Marginal pricing could eliminate an equally or more efficient competitor who lacked the ability or will to sustain losses in the short term. While not sustainable in the long run, this tactic can be economically sound and non-predatory in a variety of circumstances. Examples include reducing prices to fill excess capacity and to shift obsolescent and spoiled goods.

The sensitivity of demand to price may be such that profits are maximized at a marginal price which leaves much less than the traditional net profit. On the conventional method of pricing, such a price would probably have been considered uneconomic. Marginal pricing can therefore permit a company to adopt a far more aggressive pricing policy than a company restricted to a conventional approach to pricing.

Understanding costs is the key to low pricing
Understanding the true position of a company's costs is critical when determining prices: to set a floor, or to know how far down one can go to win the order. In fact, it is quite common for a company to complain that competitor A is selling 'below cost'. It is more likely that this is a company which is pricing aggressively, with prices well under those of reasonably well-established firms that rely on a 'full' standard cost method. Such prices may reflect an insight into profit–volume economics, or, in contrast perhaps, distress pricing. In many markets therefore there may well be good opportunities for a company which truly understands its cost structure.

Avoiding a price war
If such marginally priced work is below competitive levels, strategic judgement is required to ensure that such prices will not provoke competitive retaliation, and will not spoil the general market price levels. Marginal pricing can sometimes be interpreted by outsiders as predatory pricing, and so can precipitate a disastrous price war.

Predatory pricing
Predatory pricing, often considered unethical and illegal, refers to 'the use of short-run price cutting in an effort to exclude rivals on a basis other than efficiency in order to gain or protect market power'. Here, a firm lowers prices below average variable costs and attempts to deplete a competitor's resources and will with the hope of weakening him or putting him out of business. In most countries, predation of this sort is considered unethical, and anyway the jury is still out as to whether it works successfully. However, people do seem to believe intuitively that predation should pay while the logic of game theory appears to indicate it shouldn't.

Naturally, a predator expects to be able to recoup his expenditure, balancing the opportunity cost of temporarily reduced profits against the expectation of greater profits to come. He expects to gain market power – either by putting a competitor out of business and receiving the business, or by weakening the rival so that the cost of its acquisition is reduced. The predator's design is therefore to add the competitor's revenue to its sales and use its increased market power to increase margins.

Price predation seems to require high entry barriers to succeed – to prevent the entry of a competitor so that market power can be exercised for some period of time after the demise of the rival in order to recoup its 'investment'.

One aspect of predation is clear: the predator must have a substantial share of the market, or at least the capacity to acquire such a share. An outside observer must ask himself, 'Is the monopolist pricing low because it is engaging in predatory action or does it simply have lower costs?' This is an important consideration when a company really is pricing low because its cost base is low, as we shall see later.

Non-price predation

Companies are sometimes the subject of anti-competitive pressures not exerted through price. In fact, many of these can be used as defensive measures against a predator. Extra costs can be imposed on a competitor through legal action, government action, advertising, product innovation, or exclusionary practices such as group boycotts and price squeezes by suppliers.

Using a low cost base as a competitive weapon

'He who wishes to fight must first count the cost', wrote the sage Sun Tzu many centuries ago. It is often an expensive operation to build a business with a very low cost base. Furthermore, bringing down prices to suit can initiate a price war, which is even more expensive. However, if the process is correctly handled the lowest cost base company in the industry can win much increased demand with a lower price which still allows it to make a profit. As a by-product of increasing revenue, some competitors may choose to exit the business.

Recessions are probably the only realistic time in which this strategy of using lower costs as a competitive weapon can be carried out. In boom times, competitors tend to have a high cash flow which can fund any losses, making the attrition strategy untenable. But in recessions the profit margins and cash flow are much reduced while the risk of sustaining losses is much higher.

Vigorous competition is legal

Having a low cost base and being able to use it as a competitive weapon is an essential part of competition, preventing gross inefficiency in an industry and therefore serving the customer better. Many companies do not consider the low cost-base approach because they do not understand the ethics and laws of competition. Those that do understand can reap benefits overlooked by others.

Legislation in the Western world on pricing has been converging for many years. In the US, for example, a court ruled that 'ambitious and aggressive plans to compete, even with the goal of taking business from competitors or vanquishing a troublesome rival . . . the anti-trust laws provide no protection from such designs, where the means to effectuate them amount to no more than vigorous competition'. The law further states that it 'must not prevent a firm from pricing its goods competitively by reason of economies of scale, or the acquisition of a new efficient production facility' and that 'any successful business strategy will injure competitors to some degree'.

In Europe the Treaty of Rome and individual member countries' legislation applies. In the US the principal acts are the Robinson-Patman (1936), Sherman (1890) and Clayton (1914) Acts, accompanied by various state-wide anti-trust and loss-leader acts. They rule that 'unfair methods of competition in commerce are unlawful where the effect . . . may be to lessen competition substantially or tend to create a monopoly in any line of commerce'.

Price differences may be justified if they do no more than reflect demonstrable cost savings to the seller in dealing with particular buyers. Price differentials are also justified if they were made to meet, in good faith, the equally low price of a competitor of the seller.

Having a lower cost base than the rest

As the Japanese have shown, using cost-related price-cutting with a low cost base is one of the most viable strategies on which a sustained frontal attack can be founded. It is not a concept which can be easily emulated by a competitor: competitors can eventually work around it, and they are likely to react very aggressively if a company is perceived as acting to wipe them out. Continual improvement, or what the Japanese call *kaizen*, is essential in staying ahead of the pack. Investing in equipment and training to lower production costs can be a powerful tactic.

Arch exponents of this principle are IBM and People Express. In just five years, from 1977 to 1982, IBM poured $10 billion into plant and equipment and became acknowledged as the lowest cost producer of mainframes in its industry.

People Express. Donald C Burr, chairman of People Express (PE), achieved the lowest cost position in his industry in the early 1980s by rethinking traditional cost structures and basing his strategy on a lower cost base. 'You don't keep costs down by counting pencils and paper clips', Burr declared, 'you have to squeeze massive productivity out of people and planes.' So where the cost per seat mile for PE was just 6.66 cents, the next lowest was 7.10 cents, and the industry highest, US Air, was 11.07 cents.

> Looking at the prices charged, PE customers paid 9.3 cents, whereas US Air customers were paying 18.6 cents per mile. Hence, by aggressive cost-cutting, not only did PE have lower costs, but their prices were disproportionately low, too.

Targeting your competitors

Chess is much simpler than competitive strategy. This is even more so in emotionally charged times. Competitive opportunity requires an understanding of the impact of competitor responses to the market environment and your actions.

The low cost-base strategy requires knowledge of your costs (properly allocated) and good estimates of those of your competitors. The strategy entails working out the break-even discount (that is, how far down your prices can go) and choosing a level at which your competitor cannot cover his fixed costs or all of his variable costs. The company with the highest cost, especially the highest variable cost, is the number one target for elimination. A good understanding of relative costs of competitors and the behaviour of their variable and fixed costs is essential. It can be especially useful to watch competitors' liquidity.

In the short term, a small privately owned company might win such an expensive exercise against a multinational, since it would not be under such great pressure to achieve quarterly targets as the subsidiaries of these big companies would be. However, with the right strategic priority, and if willing to sacrifice profitability in the short term, multinationals would be more likely to win a long drawn-out contest by virtue of their greater financial resources.

Mastering competitor response

The response of your competitors will depend on where their costs are in relation to yours, whether they feel you are being deliberately aggressive towards them, and whether they can survive the effects of the attack.

To avoid competitive misunderstandings, General Electric (GE) in the US has been known in the past to share cost information with corporate visitors. 'Many of our managers have the feeling that some of our competitors don't know their real costs. And when they don't, and set prices too low, it affects our pricing also', reported a GE vice-president.

A company's ability to predict accurately the behaviour of competitors will depend on the quality of understanding of their costs and priorities. Variable cost differences may bring different responses to price drops. Typical competitor reactions are these. The prey might enter into long-term contracts with customers who might not want to see a competing supplier disappear, find financing to ride out the price-cutting, or shut down and wait for prices to rise (and re-enter later). Alternatively, it may cross-subsidize the division in your market from divisions outside (as many airlines are alleged to have done against People Express), or it may feel that it is prepared to wait, pouring money in to finance its losses, until your shareholders want higher returns and demand you raise your price.

Part IV
Buying Undervalued Companies

The following chapters describe the opportunities for buying companies and assets which tend to be undervalued because of their poor performance in the downturn.

Chapter 11 explains where the opportunities are to be found. This is a critical precursor to making the most of an acquisition, which is covered in Chapter 12.

Opportunities

This is the greatest buying opportunity . . . that I've seen in years, or may ever see.

Liedtke, chairman of Pennzoil

[When deregulation of the US oil and gas industry in the early 1980s caused a slump and companies were available at half their break-up value.]

Good time to buy cheap

Recessions provide great opportunities to buy competitors or suppliers cheaply. In fact, recessions are sometimes the only time you can do this.

The history of business is filled with examples of people who took advantage of a downturn to consolidate industries by gobbling up many small companies, or who finally rid themselves of an annoying competitor. Companies are cheaper and more available, having fallen into trouble through mismanagement, false optimism and a lack of experience. They tend to be undervalued. When the newspaper headlines are really dreadful, that is when the real bargains are picked up.

Good deals will develop

Many industrialists have voiced their opinions on the likelihood of opportunities presented by a downturn.

The US/UK company Hanson, for example, is well known for buying companies and vastly increasing their value before selling them on. A spokesman stated that Lords White and Hanson 'expect that good deals will develop out of leveraged companies'.

BTR, the acquisitive UK-based industrial conglomerate, has joined the bandwagon in stating that 'one of the pluses of a downturn is that companies will become available at good prices'.

Candover Investments, the UK's only publicly quoted investment trust specializing in buy-outs, was reported as expecting an increase in buy-out opportunities in an economic downturn.

A partner of the accountants Price Waterhouse declared himself to be surprised and delighted in early 1991 that there were 'plenty of "white knights" ready to take on an ailing business as an opportunity'.

Chapter 11

Many Cheap Companies

Understanding where the opportunities to buy companies cheaply come from requires an appreciation of the many causes of undervalued companies. It is particularly important that companies looking to buy companies and assets cheaply should avoid making the mistakes others have made in the past.

Plain incompetence

'Ninety-four per cent of company failures [are caused] by managerial incompetence', reported a study of business failures of a recession in the US. Of that, half were due to 'just plain incompetence' and the other half to 'lack of experience or unbalanced experience'. Less than 6 per cent of failures were due to 'acts of God' or external 'bad luck' factors.

Whether you agree with the extent of these figures depends on the degree of omniscience you expect of a manager. However, it is clear that many of the causes of failure we shall be considering here could have been foreseen and prepared for. It is because many instincts in a downturn are wrong that there is so much opportunity.

Getting forecasts wrong

'The forecasts made by business men are coloured by their present fortune', wrote the well-placed A C Pigou in his timely book *Industrial Fluctuations* in 1927. We all know the feeling. When everything is going up, we all have the tendency to think it will go up for ever. We project in straight lines and have real difficulty seeing change. This 'rosy scenario' syndrome is an attitude of mind which leads companies to overborrow, to gamble on stock market growth, and to have poor timing for business cycles.

A lack of realism about the fallibility of financial forecasts on which corporate borrowing is based is a major cause of corporate failure in difficult times. 'Optimistic growth assumptions', declared Charles Sanford, chief executive officer of Bankers' Trust, 'can plunge a buyer into trouble. If you look back at transactions gone bad, more often than not the problem was paying too much [on the back of an optimistic forecast].' Some analysts at credit-rating agencies even contend that any forecast beyond two years is highly unreliable. Such forecasts have led companies to vast expansion and acquisition sprees which they were later forced to watch turn sour.

In the airline industry, for example, revenues and earnings are well known for being volatile because of sudden changes in passenger traffic movements and the price of fuel. Robert Crandall, chief executive officer at American Airlines, now one of the biggest airline carriers in the world, says of his competitors that 'people seem to forget that this is a highly cyclical business'.

Overexpansion

On the expectation of greater sales in a boom time, companies have allowed their cost bases to rise. As demand fell in worsened economic conditions and increased competitive pressure, profit margins were badly squeezed. For many companies, their heavy debt didn't leave much room for a downturn. Circle K has suffered from this problem in the past. One of the largest convenience store chains in the US, Circle K was brought to the brink of filing for bankruptcy in early 1990. Its troubles stemmed from an ambitious expansion programme when it quadrupled its store base in the short space of six years. Its $1.1 billion of long-term debt weighed heavy, as did the much tougher competitive climate of those times, both of which cut into its profits.

Bad management made more obvious

Management mistakes become more exposed in difficult times. It is rather like a boat sailing up a river as the tide drops. Rocks and sandbanks become more exposed and it becomes harder to steer a true course between the rocks. In a boom, even big mistakes could be recovered from in a short time using the plentiful cash flow spun off by the business. But in the following downturn, such 'disposable income', as it is often treated, is suddenly withdrawn, leaving company strategies high and dry.

The *Financial Times*, lamenting the demise of many previous stock market 'darlings', put many of the high profile company failures down to 'youngish entrepreneurs running up against the limits of their competence'.

A good example of a company whose poor management was made more obvious by a downturn is that of Wickes.

Wickes. A celebrated Chapter 11 (see page 67) entrant of 1982, this $4 billion revenue West Coast retailer, the thirteenth largest in the US at the time, had the distinction of becoming that nation's second biggest bankruptcy. Its story is that of a race for growth leading to a major commercial misjudgement in acquiring, with a great deal of debt, a chain of stores with low potential. Such was Gamble-Skogmo, a group of 'old-town stores throughout the low-growth Mid-West', later described as having 'the wrong locations, wrong merchandise, wrong image, wrong format'. Wickes paid $200 million for Gamble-Skogmo and took on $990 million debt just before the interest rates went through the roof. Over the next two years, Wickes lost $500 million. By 1982, bills were left unpaid and suppliers refused to ship without prepayment. Wickes was forced to pay for its misjudgements by filing for protection from its creditors with debts of $2 billion.

Slim-margin businesses, such as consumer discounters, are particularly vulnerable to mistakes such as overexpansion, and can find themselves squeezed out of the market. This was the fate of the large W T Grant and E J Korvette chains in the US.

When a target releases especially poor results, that is often the time to strike. ICI, for example, coping poorly with a recession despite successive well-published bouts of restructuring, became the target of an (allegedly hostile) approach by Hanson in 1991 around the time that it became abundantly clear that its strategies had not met the earnings expectations of the stock market.

Norton is another example. In the early 1990s the Norton Company, a leading grinding and abrasives company in the US, received a $1.64 billion bid from BTR, the acquisitive British conglomerate. Big losses had been posted by Norton in 1985 and 1986, with 1988 earnings ascribed mainly to tax credits by BTR. These figures were compounded by the announcement of 'disappointing' financial performance in 1989 linked to general economic downturn. Here was a company described by a stock analyst as having excellent products and a good market position, yet it was fair for Cahill, the chief executive of BTR, to describe Norton's results as 'patchy'. It appears that it was Norton's performance before the bid, accentuated by the downturn in demand, that was the straw that broke the camel's back, giving BTR a target, putting the company 'into play', and eventually causing its sale to the French St Gobain company.

It is not just in the Western world that strategies have become unstuck. Many companies in Japan were discomfited by the world stock market crashes of October 1987 and 1989 when it became obvious that the management had let its eye stray off the ball in engaging in financial manipulations and currency dealings (termed *zaitech* by the Japanese) rather than concerning itself with core business prospects.

Inability to change

The graveyard of business is littered with companies that failed to recognize inevitable changes and adapt to them. Afflicted by such 'psychosclerosis', managers' field of action is sharply circumscribed by budgets. There is nothing so inflexible as tradition. Trapped by historical achievements, managers ignore the signals of impending crisis.

For some companies, changing a strategic plan requires almost an act of God in the boardroom, even if the basis for the original existing plan has changed. An industry observer put this down to managers' comfort in having made up their mind about a difficult issue and their concomitant reluctance to change path. Such a situation seems to have occurred in Gulf Oil.

Gulf Oil. Standard Oil/Chevron, now part of BP, acquired Gulf, the US oil company, after Gulf continued with a vastly expanded high-risk strategy when it is alleged that the shareholders' interests would have been better served in another way.

Reserves in the industry in 1982 were being consumed faster than new sources could be found. Clearly, replacing reserves was essential to long-term viability. The traditional way of doing this is to drill wildcat wells. But at that time it was more expensive to drill exploratory wells than to buy the reserves by acquiring companies in the stock market. Nevertheless James E Lee, who had become chairman of the $29 billion Gulf in 1982, expanded exploration operations, embarking on an expensive high-risk foray into the Arctic.

Forced by the downturn to slash personnel by 25 per cent and to axe many of its loss-making European operations, the company became attractive as a take-over target. Since Wall Street did not appear to appreciate Gulf's streamlining or strategic investment for the future, it was perhaps not surprising that arch corporate raider, T Boone Pickens of Mesa Petroleum, should make a bid. 'Gulf', he said, 'had a very strong balance sheet and a poor management record.' However, it was Standard Oil/Chevron which ultimately took advantage of Gulf's mistake to stick to its plan despite changed circumstances by taking over the company.

The leader can obstruct

Chief executive officers (CEOs) tend, by the very process of their selection, to be aggressive people. This often leads to their having great difficulty in admitting mistakes. When a major fall in a company's performance occurs in the changed circumstances of a downturn, the typical pattern of behaviour of the CEO tends to be a denial of the problem, then panic. The management and shareholders, realizing that the CEO is unable to give up the (now-discredited) strategy he had battled for, find themselves forced to change the CEO in order to change the strategy of their company. The chief executive can not only obstruct the change in the company's goals, but will also fight against his leaving. The removal of George Walker from his UK-quoted property and leisure vehicle Brent Walker in 1991, for example, caused a fierce struggle. For Walker, 'his life was the company and the business'. Yet the principal shareholders had decided that the turnaround of the company called for a new face – someone who had not been involved in the slide into its perilous position.

The greater fool theory

'It was fuelled by dreams – that prices would keep going up – rather than by facts. It was a boom devoid of reality . . . Rampant optimism was the order of the day,' wrote T Boone Pickens, the notorious corporate raider, about the US oil boom before the early 1980s recession.

The greater fool theory is based on the behaviour of people to buy assets and companies at elevated prices because they believe they can sell them on to an even greater fool at an even more elevated price.

Company buying sprees tend to be linked to stock market growth since much of the rationale for each is related. It was therefore no surprise that corporate acquisition activity fell after the stock market falls of 1987 and 1989. John Kenneth Galbraith drew parallels with 1929: 'People and institutions were in the market only because it was going up and they aimed to get out before it went down.'

Basing growth on continuing rise in asset values

Japanese companies and banks who used their investments in shares as collateral for ever-rising loans saw their nemesis when the stock market foundered. They were not alone in using rising asset values as the slippery foundations for ill-judged growth. Robert Crandall, chief executive officer at American Airlines (now one of the biggest airlines in the world), explains that many of his competitors 'seem to think that aircraft values keep climbing, but I've seen times when you couldn't pay someone to take an aircraft'.

Few companies budget for the extended periods of extremely high interest rates which have historically occurred in economic downturns. In boom times, easy profits more than cover interest payments, and if they get out of hand, CEOs tend to think that asset sales will provide an opportunity to cut debt. But the general lack of well-funded buyers for assets during downturns causes asset prices to tumble, leaving companies few options other than distress sales or control being given over to the banks. This provides opportunities for companies able to buy these assets.

The fate of Australian business man Alan Bond is mirrored in the collapse of the price of Van Gogh's *Irises*, a spectacular painting bought after the stock market crash of October 1987 at the spectacular price of $49 million. A short time later he was unable to find a buyer, even for the price he paid for it, and was forced to find ready cash to meet his liabilities.

Asset prices grow according to supply and demand. When cheap debt is available, then asset prices grow as the availability of debt increases. But banks' credit lines are highly dependent on their own fortunes and their confidence. When they are cut, it should be no surprise that asset values fall. Coloroll has discovered this to its cost. This UK household furnishing group in receivership is an example of a company which found that asset sales were hard to find in a seller's market. 'When times are hard', wrote the *Financial Times*, 'assets prove unreliable but liabilities remain unchanged.'

The mystique of the chief executive officer

The media and the market lionize people who manage large and growing companies.

A business man's prowess is often gauged by the size of the company he manages. Indeed, some individuals have in the past seemed to measure success as much by the size of their liabilities as by the size of their businesses.

The fastest way to increase a company's size (and liabilities) is to take over other companies. Combined with investors' demand for growth in earnings per share, the chief executive officer's ego demands lead to a never-ending growth in take-overs.

Gordon Gekko, the leading character in that archetypal boom time film *Wall Street*, exemplifies the prevalent attitude of the time with his saying: 'Greed is good.' Investment bankers exhort their clients to 'dare to be great' and inspire them to 'be all they can be'. Chief executive officers (CEOs) came to believe the hype, and the bankers came to base their judgements on the mystique of the CEO, to painful consequences, as illustrated by the Campeau and Alan Bond sagas.

'At the time it all seems perfectly plausible', declared William Mayer, head of merchant banking at First Boston, who had invested several hundreds of millions with the failed Campeau Corporation in its $6 billion take-over of Federated Department Stores on 1 April 1988. This was the deal which *Fortune* magazine described as 'the biggest looniest deal ever'. The combined company entered Chapter 11 administration on 15 January 1990. Such 'willing suspension of belief', as described with hindsight by an industry correspondent, was attributed to the mystique of the CEO himself, Robert Campeau.

Alan Bond deliberately played up to the media's swashbuckling image of him, encouraged by his financing of Australia's winning challenge in the America's Cup yacht race. He was brought down to earth by a Lonrho campaign which analyzed the complicated accounts of his holding companies. This revealed figures which made the banks nervous about Bond's abilities to cover his liabilities, with the result that the banks cut off further supplies of finance on which the whole house of cards depended. After that, Alan Bond was forced to sell assets to reduce the debt of an empire resting in the shadow of a man who had appeared larger than life.

The herd instinct

Managers have a dread of missing out on opportunities and of being pasted by their contemporaries and in published league tables. They feel they must follow the herd, even if it is going in an ultimately adverse direction.

Perhaps more compelling is the pressure that shareholders and investors place on their advisers to maximize the returns on their investments in companies. If they feel they are missing out, they will move their money elsewhere, replace senior managers, or perhaps even start a lawsuit. The risk of this happening is much reduced when everyone else is doing the same. Hence, the pressure on managers to follow short-term fashions.

The herd instinct has important ramifications for the debt levels of companies. Earnings per share growth is a typical investment criterion for a listed company and can be much increased by well-managed acquisitions. For a company whose growth has historically derived mainly from acquisitions, investors will have come to expect a certain rate of growth. This can only be achieved by more and larger acquisitions which soon exhaust the internal resources of the company, calling for external finance. Since it often takes years to pay off loans from the earnings stream, debt can accumulate rapidly. When the downturn hits, there may not be enough cash to cover the payments. The herd instinct has then claimed another victim.

Out of debt, out of danger

'If you don't want a hangover the next day,' goes the saying, 'you should not get drunk the night before.' The debt levels remaining after the dust of a whirl of acquisitions has died down are a major cause of the problems that acquirers face in a downturn. Acquirers often pay too much, a fact frequently compounded by the sheer abundance of cheap finance.

Although using debt to finance acquisitions has been a successful strategy for companies, its use requires a good understanding of its treacherous temptations.

Paying too much

Many companies have been beguiled by the same approach as the legendary art dealer Lord Duveen used when faced with the price qualms of his American millionaire clients: 'If you're buying the priceless, you're getting it cheap.'

Easy bargains in life are rare and undoubtedly vanity, an unwillingness to back down in a highly publicized bid situation, and a fear of being left behind have led chief executives to go for companies at high prices.

In the mad 1980s the size of loans seemed to be governed by the take-over price in a contested bid rather than the company's ability to repay. With investors clamouring for opportunities to invest their money, high debt levels to pay these crazy prices appeared never to have been a source of worry. 'Too much of what has happened has gone on simply because financing was available', believes an industry observer.

The 1980s were the era of financial deregulation which left too many banks chasing after too little business. In order to survive, they had to shave their margins and take greater risks. Foreign bankers wanting an entry into new markets seemed more interested in generating new business than in analyzing balance sheets. So financing was available at very low rates of interest and for more speculative schemes.

Investment bankers who earn fees based on the size of the deals, and on their reputation to set up ever bigger deals, found it in their interest to indulge the folly of their clients. Some banks were happy to win fee income from raiders whose records of managing their acquisitions ranged from 'dismal to non-existent'. Many felt, or appeared to feel, that their role was to justify any price required to top a competing offer in a contested bid.

'Caveat emptor' is arguably a fair response to criticisms of funding institutions – managers and entrepreneurs should have been aware of the capricious nature of debt. However, as a source of funding, debt can be the right choice in the right conditions.

Debt is cheaper than equity under normal conditions

Debt is well known to be able to improve returns on shareholders' equity when interest rates are not excessive. It can provide a lower cost of capital because of its tax-deductible nature, whereas dividends paid to share-holders cannot be offset against tax. So financing growth is cheaper with debt than equity. The advantages of course appear more attractive with a larger loan. Therefore, companies are tempted to take on a significant amount of debt.

The rise of the stock markets throughout the world can be partly attributed to the vast cash-flow improvements that higher borrowing has helped to generate. But leverage of this nature can be vulnerable to a downturn in business. The credit is typically taken on in the autumn of a boom, when 'rampant optimism is the order of the day'. But sales tend to fall in a downturn, while the enormous interest repayments rise, squeezing the profits. In addition, earnings are delayed, and so the cash flow required to make the interest payments is sharply reduced.

Debt forces management to realize that all cash has its price and the pressure to pay off debt when interest rates are elevated often puts 'a firecracker under management'. It commits a business to a predetermined level of performance and will not easily let up. A default in payments, or a rescheduling of debt, is a far more effective sanction of management than the forgoing of a dividend (since the shareholder base is often diffuse and without voice).

Debt therefore constrains a company in that it cannot skip interest payments, as it might if it was financed only with equity. Saatchi & Saatchi, the advertising and marketing services conglomerate, is a well-known example of a company coming under pressure from debt repayments. 'It's good to be big, its better to be good, but its best to be both,' proclaimed a Saatchi & Saatchi slogan in the early 1980s. Yet this advertising agency, which grew to become one of the world's biggest advertising agencies by a flurry of major acquisitions in just over a decade, was forced to sell several acquired companies to satisfy its debt repayments.

One of the most powerful leverage techniques in an acquisition is using the target company's assets as collateral for a loan whose interest payments will be made from the earnings of the acquired company. In this way, a minnow can develop into a whale overnight: there is no faster way to growth. Yet such an approach can more easily spawn an intractable debt problem, certainly enough to cause bankers severe heartburn.

Low threshold of pain

Bankers are those friendly people who lend you an umbrella when the sun is shining but ask for it back when clouds appear.

Lending institutions have a low threshold of pain when conditions are uncertain. Chief executives who have felt that their downside was protected by their bankers' faith in them, allowing them to roll over interest payments until asset sales could be made, or the upswing arrived, have been disappointed.

The consequences of defaulting on payment are dire. Default leads to the lenders assuming effective control of the company. 'We control your debt, we control your company', they cry. The lenders' priority tends to be above that of the shareholders: in the event of business failure, the lenders have a right to their money before the shareholders, who may have little or nothing left over. Hence, companies who have overborrowed look for ways to pay off the interest and free themselves from the pain, loss of value, loss of control, and risk they are undergoing. They will make asset sales, sell the subsidiaries, and the shareholders will accept low-priced deals to sell the whole company.

Plainly, companies need to reorganize their debt well before they have to. Laura Ashley, the UK manufacturer and retailer of women's and children's garments and house furnishings, was faced with potential debt reorganization problems which threatened its very existence. Yet they were caused by the company warning bankers of a potential problem well in advance. The company's experiences illustrate just how nervous banks can become.

The company took on a credit line to finance a £4.7 million loss from the previous year. When its debt was originally arranged in April 1988, the 11 cooperating banks were so keen to lend that they shared only £56,000 in fees between them: the interest rate margin at which they supplied money to Laura Ashley was a minuscule one-eighth of a percentage point over the rates available in the money markets.

Later, in 1990, when Laura Ashley became affected by the worsening UK trading conditions, its borrowings rose further to enable the purchase of inventory for the spring – the stores' busiest period. When it was clear that its increased gearing could put it in breach of a covenant with the banks, its management took the initiative by placing proposals for its solution on the table. People don't like to admit failure and often leave their debt reorganization, if it proves necessary, until it is too late. But here was a case of a company preparing well beforehand.

When presented with the information, many of the banks seem to have seen this as an excuse to escape their obligations and were unwilling initially to continue working with the company.

Entirely dependent on the banks' attitude for its survival, Laura Ashley was in a difficult negotiating position. A series of crises had to be endured before the situation was resolved by renegotiating gearing limits. Anne Fyfe, the group treasurer for Laura Ashley, advises companies to 'negotiate your facilities before you're anywhere near to the level whereby you risk breaching covenants. Don't even let yourself get anywhere near it.

It can happen very quickly.' She added that 'somewhere the banks lost sight of the fact that there was a company with thousands of employees at the centre of all this'. Laura Ashley's story shows that banks have a low threshold of pain and must be managed very carefully.

Mergers have high failure rates

There are more opportunities available at difficult times because of the urgency to solve cash-flow problems when the previous strategy has been found to be flawed. Yet even in good times, mergers and acquisitions have a high failure rate. One study [8] showed that, of the ten largest mergers over a decade, half of the acquiring companies would have performed worse without the merger, half better.

This failure rate is further amplified by Michael Porter of the Harvard Business School who showed that half of the acquisitions made by a group of 33 large companies were later divested, and, more critically, 74 per cent of acquisitions made in unrelated fields were later disposed of [4].

However, these figures understate the true situation, for mergers which fail to produce are not always divested because of loss of face of the management. It is widely believed by other sources that as many as 85 per cent of mergers fail to fulfil their promises of long-term profitability enhancement.

It does tend to be the conglomerates whose break-ups hit the headlines, but the reasons for smaller company break-ups appear to be similar. They include the failure to meet corporate financial performance criteria or strategic objectives; avoidance of major capital expenditure; the need to reduce corporate debt or risk exposure; the failure to generate strong cash flow; the consumption of cash faster than the company's average rate; the company's future worth is predicted to decline; the creation of a source of capital for acquisitions; or because the company is taking up too much management time for the returns generated.

Perhaps the three most important reasons for selling off subsidiaries and divisions are debt reduction (as already seen), changes in corporate strategy, and defence against take-overs. Divestiture for debt reduction is a very common feature of the upswing since companies have been holding back asset sales in the hope that the market will improve. RCA demonstrates this.

RCA. In 1981, RCA was in trouble. This $8 billion revenue company, number eight in the *Fortune* 100, was making only $54 million earnings (down from

$315 million in 1980) and had no money available for a common stock dividend.

It began to look to sell off the Hertz car rental and CIT Financial groups it had acquired two years earlier for $1.4 billion – at 80 per cent above market value. RCA also owned the NBC communications company with its large network and owned-and-operated stations. During the reign of Griffiths, its previous chairman, RCA had, according to a newspaper report, 'maintained an image of continued improvement largely by including extraordinary items and purely accounting profits in his record earnings'. The firm's troubles in the early 1980s had brought the problems to the surface. A few years later, General Electric acquired RCA for $6.3 billion.

Perkin-Elmer and American Can are examples of changes in corporate strategy leading to divestments. Perkin-Elmer represents a company which underwent a change of direction. In early 1990, it sold off its semiconductor equipment operation to the management team. An unwillingness to provide the vast amounts of money required for these operations was stated as the reason for the restructuring.

American Can Company had found that the 1980 US recession and elevated interest rates had reduced its net income by a third. It was thus only able to achieve a return on sales of less than half of that of its smaller competitor, Continental Can. It found that it was not generating enough cash to maintain its two capital-intensive businesses – cans, and wood and paper products.

With a 5 per cent growth target set by Woodside, the new chief executive officer, 'we couldn't get where we wanted to grow from where we were'. Woodside therefore decided that one division had to be sold – wood products was chosen. But wood and paper products was no dodo. It contained the well-known Dixie (paper plates and cups) company which contributed about a quarter of American Can's revenues and half of its profits.

For the company the move caused the return on assets to grow even while the assets shrank. In addition, it provided a good opportunity for a buyer to pick up a strong brand name.

Some of the spin-offs caused by the acquired company not fitting in can be highly desirable in their own right. 'Divestitures are no longer just kicking out turkeys – there is no stigma to selling an attractive division if you have a better use for the funds', reckoned a partner in a prominent investment banking firm. Perhaps that was the case with BAT.

BAT's divestiture of assets worth $3 billion after a bid by Sir James Goldsmith is a good example. BAT (formerly British American Tobacco) received a $21 billion offer from Goldsmith's Hoylake consortium in 1989. A tobacco company, BAT had used its tremendous cash flow to diversify into financial services, retailing and paper. But it was not long after the announcement of the bid that Patrick Sheehy, BAT's chief executive officer, announced plans to concentrate on tobacco and financial services. Sheehy was aware that the stock market consistently underrates diversified companies, and therefore he declared that the company would provide better shareholder value if it were split up and the constituent parts sold to their competitors in their respective industries, where these companies would pay a premium. BAT therefore reduced its interest in retailing and put the famous New York department store Saks Fifth Avenue on the block. It was eventually unloaded for $1.5 billion to Investcorp, a Bahrain-quoted investment bank. Investcorp recognized that it paid a full price but felt that it was an opportunity to snare the 'unique operating characteristics [which] add both real and intangible values in the legendary department store'. Investcorp had taken advantage of a seller's change in strategy.

Feeding frenzy

Many failed and troubled companies have suffered from the sheer speed of undigested acquisitions. FKB, a UK marketing service group, for example, owed its difficulties to buying too many companies too quickly. Its overweening debt then grew to overreach the limit of its credit facilities when the market turned down. An analyst, exasperated, declared 'they would buy one clump of companies and, before they were bedded down, they moved on to the next'.

Spinning off diversifications which didn't work

It was perhaps the unwinding of ITT, that arch exponent of diversification of the 1960s and 1970s, which highlighted the deficiencies of diversified companies. Harold Geneen, dictatorial progenitor of ITT, summed up his acquisition strategy. 'People always ask me how we selected the things we acquired: and I tell them exactly. We bought what was available.' In view of Michael Porter's finding of the difficulty of making unrelated acquisitions work [4], ITT's later divestments should have come as no surprise.

Another study [8], of almost 40 widely diversified companies over a decade, found that the average return on equity at the start was 20 per cent more than the *Fortune* 500 average. Yet at the end it was 18 per cent below the average.

The massive corporate restructuring of the 1980s was mainly driven by the hostile take-over and break-up of non-performing conglomerates to 'release shareholder value'. 'Sticking to the knitting' was the watchword of the 1980s. Many of the reasons for divestments since then remain similar. RCA, for example, then traditionally thought of as being an electronic company, purchased Coronet carpets in the 1970s with the intention that it 'should provide valuable diversification in an important consumer growth area'. A decade later it reported that 'we will consider the sale of Coronet when market conditions warrant'.

There has been a wide-ranging discussion of the merits and demerits of conglomerates for many years. Understanding the position of each side can illuminate the opportunity for acquiring companies from conglomerates which split up.

The arguments for breaking up conglomerates have ranged the whole gamut of poor financial controls, lack of management understanding of the acquired businesses, and inefficient cross-subsidies of poorly performing members of the group.

On the other hand, business risk, managers declare, is minimized in a conglomerate. Conglomerates having divisions in a range of sectors with differing sensitivities to a downturn were supposed to be highly desirable to invest in. If one company was having trading difficulties, the knowledge that it was part of a stable group would overcome wariness on the part of suppliers and customers. This was a problem experienced by Chrysler when its near-bankruptcy made headline news every day: customers were reluctant to buy product from a company which might not be around to service their automobiles in the future. The firm was forced to offer extended five-year warranties. Shareholders continue to argue, by contrast, that if they wanted to diversify their portfolios, they would split their investment across several companies.

Tax savings have provided advantages, however. A mixture of cash-hungry and cash-generating businesses can obtain group tax relief which can be used to offset profit against loss in the short term.

Synergies of shared technology, R&D, distribution and marketing were unfortunately usually overstated in the bid for greatness, and this must be a prime cause for the observed underperformance of conglomerates.

Stock analysts often specialize in sectors. However, information on the performance of consolidated subsidiaries is hard to come by. This is because less information is required by the authorities to be disclosed for a holding company's constituent parts. It is therefore harder for an outside observer to place a realistic value. This is believed to be one reason why diversified companies tend to be undervalued compared to the sectors of their subsidiaries.

Some observers believe the impetus for divestment in the 1990s will be modified to come from three quarters. There will be unprecedented organizational and strategic complexities from competing with global rivals. The nature and degree of these challenges will vary a great deal across businesses. More importantly, it is likely that the style of corporate governance, or 'parenting', to cope with these challenges will vary widely. When these factors are combined it is expected that divestments will increase.

Disintegration

Some companies are finding that extensive vertical integration has been using too much management time and makes the company too unwieldy. Hence, many integrated companies are being split up. This is of course a cycle which has repeated itself in history. For instance, media magnates used to own paper mills and the forests to supply them, and tyre manufacturers controlled the plantations for their raw material. Henry Ford even had a sheep farm to grow wool for car seat covers. This is the case no longer.

Overcapacity

Periods of overcapacity lead to remarkable drops in price which can provide opportunities. Shipping is a prime example. With its high fixed costs, considerable time-lag between ordering and receiving ships, and a volatile market, owning ships for transport is a cyclical business of great swings. A previous shipping slump, for example, was so bad that ships were being sold for scrap at just 15 per cent of their original purchase price of a few years before.

Several companies have exploited such swings opportunistically. It was reportedly part of the cut-price airline, People Express's, strategy that the company should buy airplanes cheaply in a period of overcapacity. ODECO in the US has purchased oil rigs during downturns, when prices are depressed, as part of its cost leadership strategy. Thyssen, the large German steel manufacturer, makes speciality steels whose costs are vulnerable to wild fluctuations of alloy prices. At one time, molybdenum, which is used to strengthen steel, doubled in price. Thyssen was reported as having built up large strategic stockpiles of molybdenum to guard against just such an occurrence.

Buying abroad

Opportunities to buy companies and assets cheaply are also available to companies that are able to buy into such markets when they are in a downturn. Southland Corporation, for example, long-time owners of the '7-11' convenience store chain, had been in financial difficulties. The Japanese '7-11' companies took advantage of this and bought up 75 per cent of the US companies, assuming all the parent's debt.

As capital becomes increasingly available and financial institutions become increasingly active across borders, companies become much more vulnerable, even those of much greater size than their predators. More companies are also becoming available for sale. In Europe, for example, many companies founded in the years after the Second World War are up for sale as founders reach retirement age.

Small wonder that it was recently discovered that 84 per cent of European chief executives are planning to expand internationally across borders by merger and acquisition over the next decade. This is aided by the fact that regulatory authorities are clarifying and, in some cases, easing their attitude towards acquisitions.

Different accounting procedures in different nations have also been a substantial source of opportunity. Both Japanese and UK companies have been heavily engaged in a buying spree in the US for many years, typically paying 15–20 per cent above what an American would pay. For the Japanese, these high prices could be justified either by their tax losses or when compared to the high price–earnings ratios of their home stock market.

For the British, cross-border accounting differences are usually attributed to their ability to pay high. 'The US', reported Sanford Pengler in the *Wall Street Journal*, 'requires the amortization of the goodwill representing the premium paid over the hard asset value of a firm. In Britain, goodwill can be carried for ever on the balance sheet. The improved after-tax cash flow which results helps the foreign firm bid higher than a US counterpart could.'

Mitchell Fromstein, chief executive officer of Manpower, once displaced by such a deal, was exasperated by the situation. 'Blue Arrow wrote off $1 billion in goodwill on a $1.3 billion purchase price in one stroke. The [UK] stock market looked at it for a day, then forgot it. But in the US you'd have to write it off at $30 million a year without a tax benefit.'

The liberal nature of the UK accountancy rules encouraged these companies to boost short-term earnings by making more acquisitions.

Exploiting tax losses

Companies which have made losses can be acquired as tax losses which can be offset against future profits to reduce tax bills. This is another example of effectively buying a profit stream at a discount.

Occidental Petroleum, whose chairman was Armand Hammer, made an offer of equity exchange in 1981 for Iowa Beef, a low-cost beef processor. Apart from the ability to absorb about $117 million of tax credits, this had the potential of hedging against economic downturn.

In 1980, Baldwin, the chief executive officer of **United Insurance** (a $1.6 billion company in 1981), arranged to buy a Californian insurance company with $20 million unrealized tax losses in its loans portfolio. That bought him two years of tax credits. Using this strategy, Baldwin was able to avoid paying taxes higher than 15 per cent of the company's net income for some time.

Chapter 12

Making the Most of the Buying Opportunity

Why do companies buy others? Because their management can see inefficiencies everywhere, and opportunities for enriching themselves and their investors by streamlining their acquisitions.

This chapter examines various opportunities for realizing the full value of acquisitions and makes suggestions on how to manage the process of acquisition successfully.

Undervalued companies

Profit stream at a discount

The main reason why companies are acquired is to buy the profit stream at a discount; that is, the acquirer will get more out than he puts in. The seller sells because he feels that he can get more money from the buyer than he can get from the company itself or because he needs to realize his investment quickly to meet his other liabilities.

The profit an acquirer will make on his investment will come from spotting undervalued assets or companies, or because something extra is brought to the party. The fact that vendors often have their backs against the wall when negotiating a divestment in difficult times will reduce the amount a company should have to pay. Furthermore, the anti-trust and monopolies regulatory authorities tend to be more lenient in tough times when it appears many jobs and votes are at stake if the deal falls through.

Identifying assets which could fetch more than was paid for them is the very essence of trading.

So many companies have been so poorly managed and valued that several companies have taken advantage of the opportunity by concentrating on buying cheaply as their main activity. Sometimes disparaged as 'asset-strippers', they have made significant profits by releasing shareholder value. It could also be argued that they perform a valuable function by forcing world industry to use its assets more effectively. Perhaps the two best known of these acquirers are Hanson and Goldsmith. They have managed to find companies so undervalued and undermanaged that they have been able to buy businesses and sell off relatively minor divisions and yet leave a residual value almost as much as was originally paid. Deals such as Imperial Tobacco and Crown Zellerbach forests come to mind.

Diversified companies whose constituent companies reap little benefit from the other companies in the group are often undervalued by the stock markets. Parts can detract from one another, both because of the deadening effect of bureaucracy and because winners subsidize losers. Another reason why their stock trades under their break-up value is because investors realize that the competitors of the constituent companies will pay a premium for them, since they can derive more value by integrating them with their companies. Hence, conglomerates and diversified companies are being forced to sell divisions before take-over merchants get to work on them.

As companies take on debt, they often invite predatory behaviour from their rivals. Difficulties with paying their debt will therefore make companies vulnerable to acquisition. The fact that so many companies in the US food retail sector are hocked to their eyebrows enabled A&P, one of the few larger supermarket firms with a clean balance sheet, to expand aggressively into their markets, with barely a whimper from its rivals.

When target company prices had fallen some 20 per cent by 1990 in under one year the influential 'Lex' column of the *Financial Times* was moved to comment that 'take-overs are again being driven increasingly by strategic and commercial reasons rather than financial anomalies'. Another newspaper reported that the 'sharp drop in the value of speculative take-over stocks is a feature of the market on both sides of the Atlantic'. When the crazy prices of the boom times come back down to earth, it often happens that companies are undervalued, especially if you can take the long-term view.

In simplistic terms, a firm's worth can be seen as no more than the sum of the profit stream into the future (suitably discounted for inflation, value of money, risk, etc). Estimating the profit stream usually starts by projecting performance into the future. Owing to the nature of human psychology, as we have seen, forecasts are heavily dependent on the present situation. So, in essence, projections tend to consist of straight lines.

A company with recent poor performance would have a perceived low net worth. But underperformance may be due to the cyclical nature of the market, in which case the long-term value is considerably higher. On stock markets, this is indicated by a noticeable drop in the price/earnings ratio at the onset of a downturn. So companies' profit streams become cheaper to buy in a recession. Some managements take advantage of this by buying back their own shares.

Similarly, a company making losses could appear to have a negative worth. Such companies can therefore be given away. Some investors will even pay you to take the company off their hands if the management see the haemorrhaging as uncontrollable.

Fortune favours the brave

Some of the best deals are opportunities which need strong nerves, and there are a great many about in difficult times. 'This is a wonderful time to scavenge', wrote an investment fund manager, 'for the supply of [distressed and bankrupt] companies is large and growing.'

One way to take control of a company is to buy its distressed debt and to use this, rather than a shareholding, to gain control or make a favourable deal with the managers. Indeed, the scale of losses on corporate debt in a downturn makes people trade much of the debt like equity. 'An instrument which yields 15 per cent is clearly a debt instrument. A 30 per cent yield tells you that payments and redemption may not be timely and that has to be treated as an equity-type investment', reported a director of research at a well-known Wall Street firm.

Bankrupt companies or those close to receivership or Chapter 11 administration can be good deals. The advent of increased legal liabilities for directors who continue to trade while their company is technically bankrupt has tended to ensure that failing companies file for protection from their creditors through Chapter 11 administration or its equivalent much sooner than before. For such acquisitions, getting access to the 'deal flow' is critical. Information on weak companies can be found from accountants, lawyers, investment banks and public filings from company examinees and trustees.

There are also several well-known methods for predicting the failure of a company. Examples are the much used Z and Zeta scores (for public and private companies respectively) developed by Edward Altman, the acknowledged guru of this field, in his book, *Corporate Financial Distress*. They can be good indicators of opportunity if applied early enough.

A good example of making the most of bankrupt and near-bankrupt companies is that of IBH.

IBH. It was in Germany that Horst-Dieter Esch built his company, IBH (Internationale Baumaschinen Holding), to become the world's number three construction equipment company (at that time – the early 1980s) by initially buying the industry's 'walking wounded'. Esch was well known for buying companies for next to nothing.

He took over the small German family firm of Zettelmeyer, a victim of the 1974–5 recession, saying he would pay for it when he had seen from the inside how much it was worth. His due diligence convinced him that he should pay nothing for the company, and he took control. His next three firms were acquired for nothing, for a token amount, and for $250,000.

He had soon acquired critical mass and large companies offered him their money-losing operations. In 1979 he acquired three divisions from a French company for nothing. He later bought General Motors' Terex, a leading construction equipment company, on a long-term note.

In this way, Esch was able to construct a company with 7 per cent of the world's market, behind only Caterpillar and Komatsu, and ahead of Deere, Massey-Ferguson and Fiat-Allis.

Unfortunately, Esch and IBH were to suffer in the recession which followed when his opportunistic deal-making skills were insufficient to survive a market collapse.

That fortune favours the brave can be seen in this story of the Reichmanns.

The Reichmann brothers were considered by *Forbes* magazine in 1991 to be the seventh richest people in the world. They made their fortune from property; their company, Olympia and York, is well known for having expanded in market troughs. In 1977, they snapped up a package of eight Manhattan office towers for $320 million just when the rental market scraped bottom. Their value had grown to nearly $3 billion by 1982, providing considerable borrowing clout for further expansion.

Realizing the value of an acquisition

Bringing something to the party

We have already discussed one of the ways of making money on an acquisition: buying it at an undervalued price. But such bargains are rare and most companies will have to make their profits the hard way; that is, by working to improve the value of the company.

Bringing something to the party can be either managerial expertise, financial resources, or another company with which to integrate the newly acquired. Companies such as Hanson buy others, inject strict financial disciplines, apply ruthless cost-cutting, invest only in well-targeted areas, and then sell the companies on after three or four years if the value they can win in the marketplace exceeds their estimate of their net worth.

Companies which do not have the capital resources to develop, for example, a new technology can agree to be acquired by a larger combine which can provide that missing element. Genentech, the prominent biotechnology company, for example, was bought into by Rhône-Poulenc, the large French pharmaceutical combine in 1990, in order to provide Genentech with access to Rhône-Poulenc's finance and a distribution network for its revolutionary products.

Integrating one company with another can provide unlocked access to the market, increased market power, and the potential of lower costs. For brand names and access to exclusive channels, a merger often proves to be quicker and cheaper than starting from scratch. Sometimes the alternative may be too expensive to be worthwhile at all.

Greater market power

PIMS (Profit Impact of Market Strategy), a long-running database of the performance of companies held by the Harvard Business School, shows that, provided the market is defined properly (by finding little sign of overlaps of costs, customers or competitors across neighbouring segments), a larger market share gives the potential for greater profit margins. One of the reasons for this arises from the greater negotiating power derived from greater size. This means better prices and preferred access, which can be used as an entry barrier.

A higher profile among the financial community can help in raising money. A more prominent market position helps with customer recognition and, as a side-effect, can substantially aid recruiting where people tend to go for a name they recognize.

Cost savings

One of the most important reasons for acquisition is saving money by having reduced costs. Unfortunately, it is also the most abused: the inability of management to turn its potential into reality is a prime cause of acquisitions failing to meet expectations. Too many companies cite cost savings when paying a large premium for a company, yet they have not thought hard about where the savings are going to come from. If rationalization within a firm makes sense, then it should make even more sense in synergies between two firms.

There are several ways of reducing costs and therefore releasing money directly on to the bottom line. These are cost sharing, higher capacity utilization, being more efficient because of greater scale, and because the organization learns how to do things more efficiently as it produces more. Bringing profits in-house by vertical integration is another possibility.

Sharing fixed costs

Sharing costs by combining companies is a common desire. Having one sales-force carry two product ranges to each customer instead of two sales-forces operating separately is one example.

A further example of sharing fixed costs is the avoidance of duplication of effort that one instead of two R&D departments can produce; that is, the effort is shared by both the companies and spread over the revenues of the combined companies. Continental, the German tyre company, for example, and Pirelli, its Italian rival, have held extended merger talks in the past. The reason is that a merger, if well handled, could save the combined company a great deal of money on production, distribution and R&D. Separately, the tyre companies may have difficulties making ends meet in competing with their larger global competitors.

Improved capacity utilization also uses the principle of sharing costs. For example, in an industry with high fixed costs, such as food processing, combining two plants which are both below capacity will give much better capacity utilization, and the costs will be released as profits directly on to the bottom line.

Buying a company and closing it down to remove excess capacity from the market is another idea.

Economies of scale

Economies of scale derive from being more efficient because of higher throughput. It is often the case that one large plant at full capacity is more efficient than several smaller plants also at maximum capacity. The reasons for this may include reduced transport costs, less administration costs and better prices when bargaining for materials.

Vertical integration

We tend to think about buying competitors but it may be advantageous to buy control of some suppliers or customers. Such a vertical integration strategy, whereby the middleman transaction costs are internalized, can be made substantially cheaper by a downturn. This may also be a useful strategy for circumventing a dominant supplier. However, you need to be aware of the arguments, mentioned in the previous chapter, concerning the usually unexpected amount of management time and change of focus caused by making such an acquisition.

US Steel is a well-publicized example of integration both vertically (among suppliers) and horizontally (among product groups). Its highly successful consolidation of the US steel industry at the turn of the century demonstrates the lower costs which can come from better utilization, scale economies and experience effects.

The experience curve

Organizations improving over time as they learn how to do a job better provide another source of cost saving. Related to the well-known learning curve, where people become more efficient the more they practise, is the so-called 'experience curve'. This describes the potential fall in costs as the cumulative number of units produced increases, provided the process is aggressively managed. This is an empirically derived relationship which really holds true in many industries.

Anyone who doubts the existence of such a relationship should talk to a manager of a place of work where piece-work rates have been based on the completion times for the first handfuls of a new product, or the first few hours of a new process. It won't be long before the workers will be legitimately earning double the estimated weekly pay, since they will have learned to make twice as many products in the same time.

When this concept has been correctly applied to companies, it has been able to produce a reduction in the unit cost of a product over time. One way the experience curve is used is to justify acquisitions to increase market share, which, since there are more units passing through, has the potential to cause a decrease in unit costs faster. Alternatively, since the potential cost reduction can be reasonably well forecast against volume, some companies have deliberately priced very low with a new product in order to stimulate demand, which brings lower unit costs and increased profit margins.

Managing the acquisition process successfully

When to buy

'In theory, the ideal time to cherry-pick is in the depths of a recession, after the stock market craters,' reported a leader in the *Wall Street Journal*. That is the opinion of the proponents of the 'early bird catches the worm' principle. Others, of the 'darkest hour is just before dawn' school, feel that you should wait until a little later, when you can see the light at the end of the tunnel.

While prices will clearly be cheaper when immediate prospects appear poor and cash flow is minimal, this has to be balanced against the cost of carrying an ailing company until it emerges into the broad sunlit uplands, the management time required by the host company's business, and, importantly, whether bankers can be persuaded to lend money to finance the deal. Being human, they too are subject to straight-line forecasting tendencies and tend to be chastened by their free lending in the previous boom time.

In review, my opinion is that companies should think about buying as soon as their business has been secured, can spare the management time, and can raise the resources. Towards the end of a difficult period, you're leaner, they're leaner, the risk of further failure of demand has been limited, and it is easier to raise finance. Buying undervalued and underperforming companies is a major opportunity in a downturn. It would be a shame to miss out. However, maximizing the opportunity is important. A few reminders of the key success factors in an acquisition or merger are presented here.

Value correctly

Consider where the cost savings and increased market power are really going to come from. If they are real, then you should be able to put a figure on its value. However, when valuing the company, be conservative in your estimates of market demand – ensure that you can cope with the worst case.

The target company often overstates its future expected growth in order to increase its bidding value. This needs to be allowed for. Leasing companies, for example, are notorious for using unusual interpretations of the financial reporting regulations.

Get the true story. Perform 'due diligence' on the target company, if you can. Crawl inside the company and find the real figures and the good management. This avoids nasty surprises.

After a difficult period through which companies have struggled hard and their bad management has been shown up, there does tend to be an increased prevalence of fraud as past deeds are covered up. The accounts, as seen in several important cases in the early 1990s, do not always shed much light or even provide any clue.

We have seen that paying too much has often been a major cause of the failure of an acquisition to meet expectations. A key way of avoiding this is to value the company and calculate the 'walk-away price': the price beyond which you cannot make an acceptable return and which you will not allow yourself to overstep.

Cultural aspects are critical

The financial and marketing aspects are traditionally considered first in an acquisition, and sometimes to the exclusion of all other considerations. However, so many acquisitions fail because of cultural differences between companies and their top managements. Hence, cultural aspects should be seen as critical to the success of the venture. There are numerous examples of mergers between East and West Coast companies in the US, for example, which have failed for this very reason.

Agreed bids are cheaper than hostile bids

Agreed bids require less premium the hard asset value and over the market price. Studies throughout the 1980s showed that the premium over hard assets required for agreed bids was half that of hostile bids. Hence, considerable effort should be expended in maintaining cordial relations.

Interestingly, unlike the impressions fostered by the media, a study showed that the vast majority of acquisitions are in fact quiet, amicable affairs. When the difference between hostile and agreed approaches is likened to the difference between rape and courtship, it makes sense to approach the target company in a non-aggressive fashion and to be open about the benefits on both sides.

Defer payment

One of the best insurance policies against potential problems is to pay in deferred tranches. By making top managers and founders agree to the objectives, and basing their reward on performance in achieving them, they remain highly motivated to stay and do a good job. Advertising and software are sectors which are well known for their use of such an 'earn-out' policy. It is particularly important for them when, as the saying goes, the company's assets go out the door at the end of each day.

Have a plan

Before signing on the dotted line, you must have a plan, and you must communicate it widely. If you don't, management will march to the beat of different drummers, or as the Japanese say 'share a bed but dream different dreams'. Without a plan, all-important timing can all too easily slip out of control in the confusion.

Examining the annual filings of acquisitive companies invariably turns up a director's comment that 'difficulties with an acquisition have depressed profits'. Apart from strategic reasons, many mergers fail to reach their expected return because they were either not integrated quickly, or not at all. A plan is critical.

Act quickly

Cuts in personnel and operations should be made quickly. In this way, the organization can make a fresh start: personnel do not spend their time worrying about their security and becoming involved in machinations to undermine your efforts. Decisions on what and whom to axe should be near-complete before entering the acquired company, if possible. Some firms have a 'flying squad' which very quickly collects vital information in the week after formal signing-over, and decisions are finalized over the following weekend.

The need to act quickly does not end a week or two after the acquisition. The merged entity must now be pushed towards those objectives of the deal which justified the price. Problems on the way need to be dealt with rapidly.

Many international marketing services companies, for example, have experienced problems in the past with their acquisitions when they reached a downturn where conditions changed rapidly.

Indeed the relative resilience of Shandwick (the UK PR and marketing services firm) owes a great deal to its installing financial systems which allow the company to spot and rectify problems quickly, and its quickly bringing in experienced managers as it grew.

It is important that communications should always remain cordial. 'Friendly but not too friendly' is how one turnaround manager described his idea of the right attitude. Naturally, a merger is a form of relationship and you have to work with these people in the future, but this must be balanced against allowing dead wood to survive for sentimental reasons.

Conclusion

We reach the end of a journey in which a company has exploited the three important forms of competitive opportunity presented by a downturn. By reducing costs, becoming more flexible and freeing up flows of cash, it has become a formidable, lean and hungry machine. By using improved marketing techniques, the firm has been able to wrong-foot competitors and build a foundation for greater market power in the future. In addition, the cash saved can be used for other battles in acquiring companies and assets inexpensively.

References

[1] 'Industrial Pricing: Strategy vs Tactics', Robert Garda, *McKinsey Quarterly*, Winter 1984.

[2] 'Overmanning: Germany vs Britain', *Management Today*, August 1981, p.43.

[3] *Economist*, 29 June 1991, p.28.

[4] 'From Competitive Advantage to Corporate Strategy', Michael E Porter, *Harvard Business Review*, May–June 1987, p.44.

[5] *How Advertising in Recession Periods Affects Sales*, American Business Press Inc, 1979.

[6] 'Advertising as an Anti-recession Tool', Nariman K Dhalla, *Harvard Business Review*, Jan–Feb 1980, pp.159–165.

[7] *The Generation of Ideas for New Products*, Trevor Sowrey, Kogan Page, 1987.

[8] 'The Agonies of Agglomeration', *Management Today*, Feb 1986, p.42.

Further Reading

American Steel, Richard Preston, Prentice-Hall, 1991.
Competitive Advantage, Michael E Porter, Collier Macmillan, 1985.
Corporate Financial Distress (A complete guide to predicting, avoiding and dealing with bankruptcy), Edward I Altman, Wiley, 1983.
Economics, Paul A Samuelson and William D Nordhaus, McGraw-Hill, 1985.
Economics of Trade Unions, Albert Rees, Nisbet, 1962.
In Search of Excellence, Tom Peters, Harper and Row, 1983.
Industrial Fluctuations, A C Pigou, F Cass, 1968.
Managing Knowhow, Karl E Sveiby and Tom Lloyd, Bloomsbury, 1987.
'Marketing Success through Differentiation – of Anything', Theodore Levitt, *Harvard Business Review*, Jan–Feb 1980, pp.83–91.
Marketing Technology: An Insider's View, William H Davidson, Free Press, 1986.
The Mind of the Strategist, Kenichi Ohmae, McGraw-Hill, 1982; Penguin 1987.
Moments of Truth, Jan Carlzon, Ballinger Publishing/Harper & Row, 1987.

A complete list of Kogan Page management titles is available from the publisher at 120 Pentonville Road, London N1 9JN; telephone 071-278 0433.

Index